The vet. book : an account of the ailments of and accidents to domestic animals

Frank Townend Barton b. 1869

Nabu Public Domain Reprints:

You are holding a reproduction of an original work published before 1923 that is in the public domain in the United States of America, and possibly other countries. You may freely copy and distribute this work as no entity (individual or corporate) has a copyright on the body of the work. This book may contain prior copyright references, and library stamps (as most of these works were scanned from library copies). These have been scanned and retained as part of the historical artifact.

This book may have occasional imperfections such as missing or blurred pages, poor pictures, errant marks, etc. that were either part of the original artifact, or were introduced by the scanning process. We believe this work is culturally important, and despite the imperfections, have elected to bring it back into print as part of our continuing commitment to the preservation of printed works worldwide. We appreciate your understanding of the imperfections in the preservation process, and hope you enjoy this valuable book.

Webster Family Library of Veterinary Medicine
Cummings School of Veterinary Medicine at
Tufts University
200 Westboro Road

THE COUNTRY HANDBOOKS
Edited by Harry Roberts

The Vet. Book

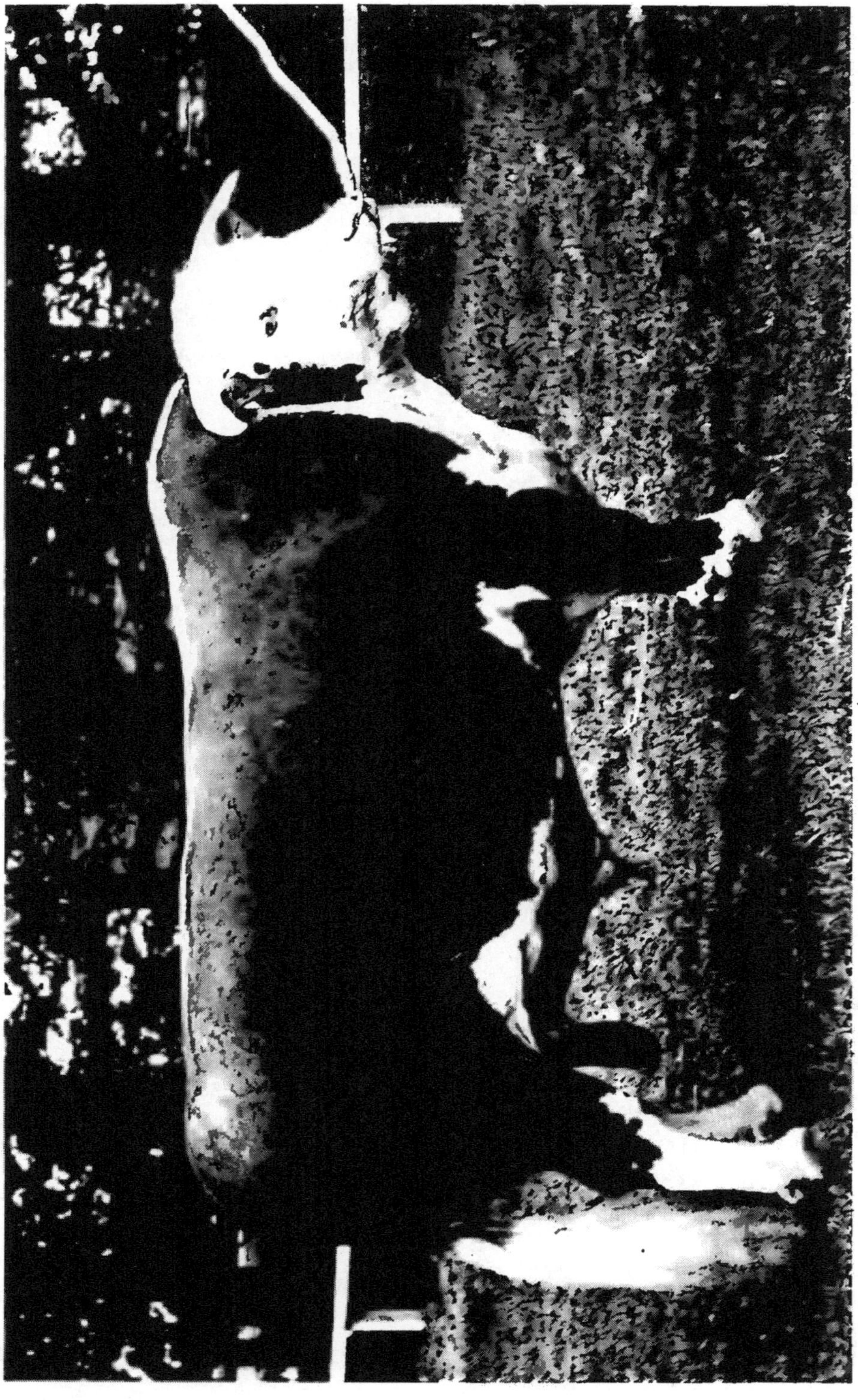

The Vet. Book
An Account of the Ailments of and Accidents to Domestic Animals, by
Frank Townend Barton
M.R.C.V.S.

London: John Lane, The Bodley Head
New York: John Lane Company

Turnbull & Spears, Printers, Edinburgh

Note

THE Author in presenting this small guide has endeavoured to give a brief and practical account of the commoner ailments and accidents incidental to the horse, ox, sheep, pig, dog, cat, etc., etc., and when necessary, has indicated the lines of treatment and management to be adopted in cases of emergency. The reader must understand that professional aid is, in the majority of instances, the most economical after all, because of the uncertainty confronting the amateur in the diagnosing of disease, which may lead to the application of remedies altogether unsuitable, to say nothing of the risk involved and the dangers attending the misapplication of any given remedy.

[Thanks are due to the Board of Agriculture for permission to reproduce four illustrations from the leaflets issued by them. Thanks are also due to the Proprietors of the *Chemist and Druggist*, for permission to reproduce some illustrations from their excellent publications.—ED.]

Contents

	Page
EDITOR'S NOTE	v
INTRODUCTION TO THE STUDY OF DISEASE . . .	xvii
The Pulse	x
The Temperature	xiii
The Respirations	xv
Mucous Membranes	xvi
Age and Sex	xvii
Surroundings	xviii
Heredity	xix
Specific or Germ Diseases . . .	xx
Influence of Soil, Climate, etc. . . .	xxiii

CHAPTER I

ANATOMICAL RUDIMENTS OF DOMESTIC ANIMALS . .	1
The Horse	1
The Ox, Sheep, and Goat . . .	11
The Pig	16
The Dog and the Cat	17
The Fowl	19

CHAPTER II

GENERAL MANAGEMENT IN DISEASE . . .	21
Administering Medicines	21
Feeding Sick Animals	25
Nursing	26
Fomentations and Poultices . . .	28

The Vet. Book

GENERAL MANAGEMENT IN DISEASE—*continued*. Page

The Cautery and Blistering Agents . . 30
The Slings; Cradle; and Hobbles . . . 32

A

Abortion 33
Abdominal Dropsy 36
Abdominal Tumours 36
Abscess 37
Actinomycosis (Timber Tongue) . . . 38
Acute Congestion of the Lungs . . . 39
Acute Inflammation of the Kidneys . . 40
Acute Scour in Foals, Lambs, and Calves . . 40
Amaurosis 42
Anchylosis 42
Anemia 43
Angleberries (*see* Warts) 43
Anthrax 43
Aphtha 46
Apoplexy of the Lungs (*see* Congestion of Lungs) . 46
Apoplexy, Parturient (*see* Parturient Apoplexy) . 46
Apoplexy of the Brain 46
Arteries, Injuries to (*see* Wounds) . . . 46
Arsenical Poisoning 46
Ascarides (*see* Worms) 47
Asthma 47

B

Belladonna 48
Bites and Stings 48
Bladder, Inflammation of 49
Bladder, Stone within 49
Bleeding 50
Bloody Flux (*see* Dysentery) 50
Blood Poisoning 50
Blood Spavin (*see* Bone Spavin) . . . 51
Bog Spavin 51

Contents

GENERAL MANAGEMENT IN DISEASE—*continued.*	*Page*
Bone Spavin	51
Bots	53
Bowels, Inflammation of	54
Braxy	55
Broken Wind	56
Broken Knees (*see* Wounds)	57
Bronchitis	57
Bruises	58
Burns	59
Bursal Enlargements (Windgall, etc.)	59

C

Canker of the Foot	60
Canker of the Ear	61
Capped Elbow	62
Capped Hock (*see* Hocks, Capped)	62
Cartilages, Ossified (*see* Side Bone)	62
Cataract	63
Catarrh	63
Chest Founder	64
Chapped Heels	64
Chorea (Twitch, Jumps, St Vitus' Dance)	65
Chronic Cough	65
Coffin Bone (Fractured)	65
Colic (*see* Gripes)	65
Concretions in the Intestines	66
Contracted Feet	66
Corns	67
Crib-Biting	67
Curb	68
Cutting	68

D

Depraved Appetite	69
Diabetes	69
Diarrhœa	70

The Vet. Book

GENERAL MANAGEMENT IN DISEASE—*continued.*   *Page*

    Dislocations 71
    Distemper (Influenza in Horse) . . . 71
    Dysentery 74

E

    Eczema 75
    Enteritis (*see* Abdominal Pain) . . . 76
    Epilepsy 76
    Erythema (Sore Shoulders, Saddle Galls, etc.) . 77
    Eye (*see* Inflammation of) 78
    Eyelids, Torn (*see* Wounds) . . . 78

F

    Falling of the Womb (*see* Prolapsus Uteri) . 78
    False Quarter 78
    Farcy (*see* Glanders) 78
    Fetlock Joint (Sprain of) 78
    Fistula (*see* Withers) 79
    Flatulent Colic (*see also* Gripes) . . . 79
    Flexor Tendon (Sprain of) 79
    Fluke Disease (see Liver-rot) . . . 80
    Foot Punctured 80
    Foot-rot and Foul 80
    Founder of Feet (*see* Laminitis) . . . 82
    Fractures 82

G

    Gangrene 83
    Gapes 84
    Glanders 85
    Grease 86
    Glossitis (Inflammation of Tongue) . . 87
    Gripes (or Colic) 87

H

    Hæmaturia 88
    Hæmorrhage 88

Contents

GENERAL MANAGEMENT IN DISEASE—*continued.*   *Page*

    Hæmorrhoids (Piles) 90
    Heart (Affections of) 90
    Herniæ (*see* Ruptures) 90
    Hip (Injuries to) 90
    Hocks (Capped) 91
    Hock-Joint, Open (*see* Joint, Open) . . 92
    Hoven (Dew-blown) = Tympanitis . . 92
    Husk or Hoose 94

I

Indigestion 95
Inflammation of the Bowels (*see* Bowels) . . 95
Inflammation of Udder (*see* Mammitis) . . 95
Inflammation of Lungs (*see* Pneumonia) . . 95
Inflammation of the Eye 95
Itch (*see* Mange) 96

J

Jaundice (the Yellows) 96
Joint, Open 97

K

Kidneys (*see* Acute Inflammation of) . . 98

L

Laminitis (Founder of the Feet) . . . 98
Laryngitis (*see* Sore Throat) . . . 100
Legs, Swollen (Œdema) 100
Leg-Weakness in Poultry 100
Lice 101
Liver-rot (or Fluke) 101
Lock-jaw (Tetanus) 103
Lymphangitis (*see* Weed) 104

GENERAL MANAGEMENT IN DISEASE—*continued.* Page

M

Maggots in Sheep (*see* Wounds)	105
Mammitis (*see* Udder)	105
Mange	105
Megrims (Vertigo)	108
Mortification (*see* Gangrene)	108
Moulting	108

N

Navicular Disease	109
Navel Ill	110

O

Ophthalmia (*see* Inflammation of Eye)	110
Over-reach	110

P

Paralysis	111
Parasites, Internal, in Sheep (*see* Worms)	112
Parturient Apoplexy (Milk Fever)	112
Peritonitis (*see* Inflammation of Bowels)	113
Piles (*see* Hæmorrhoids)	113
Pleurisy	114
Pneumonia	114
Poisoning	115
Prolapsus Uteri (Falling of Womb), also Prolapsus Ani, etc.	116
Psoriasis (*see* Eczema)	117
Pyæmia (*see* Blood Poisoning)	117

R

Rabies	117
Red-Water and Black-Water	118
Rheumatism, Chest Founder, or Kennel Lameness	119

Contents

GENERAL MANAGEMENT IN DISEASE—*continued.*   *Page*

Ribs (*see* Fractures)	120
Rickets	120
Rinderpest (or Cattle Plague, Murrain)	121
Ringworm	121
Ring-bone	121
Roaring	122
Ruptures	123
Roup	124

S

Sand Crack	125
Scabies and Sheep Scab (*see* Mange)	126
Scour (*see* Acute Scour, also Diarrhœa)	126
Sore Throat	126
Staggers	126
Stiff Joint (*see* Anchylosis)	126
Side Bone	127
Splint	127
Strangles	129
Sturdy (Turn-Sick or Gid)	130
Swelled Legs (*see* Legs, Swollen)	131
Swine Fever	131

T

Teats (Soreness of)	132
Teats Impervious	133
Tetanus (*see* Lock-jaw)	133
Tuberculosis (Consumption)	133
Tympanitis (*see* Hoven)	135

U

Udder, Inflammation of (Garget)	135
Urine, Blood in (*see* Hæmaturia)	136
Urticaria (or Nettle-rash)	136
Uterus, Inversion of (*see* Prolapsus Uteri)	136

V

Vertigo (Giddiness)	136

The Vet. Book

GENERAL MANAGEMENT IN DISEASE—*continued.*   Page

W

Warts	137
Wind, Broken (*see* Broken Wind)	137
Wind Galls (*see* Bursal Enlargements)	137
Weed (Lymphangitis)	137
Worms	138
Wounds	140

Y

Yew-tree Poisoning (*see* Poisoning)	143

List of Illustrations

HEREFORD BULL—FIRE KING	*Frontispiece*
	Page
THE EXTERIOR OF THE HORSE	2
PARTS OF THE HORSE	4
SEATS OF DISEASE IN HORSE'S HIND LEG	6
SEATS OF DISEASES IN THE HORSE	8
FOOT OF HORSE	10
HEART AND STOMACH OF THE OX	12
THE EXTERIOR OF THE COW	14
PARTS OF THE OX	15
FOWL LOUSE (*Gon. hologaster*)	18
FEATHER-EATING SCABIES	18
FOWL LOUSE (*Men. pallidum*)	19
FOWL LOUSE (*Lip. variabilis*)	19
COTSWOLD RAM	*To face* 22
DRENCHING A PIG	22
A TYPICAL SHORTHORN BULL	*To face* 40
BOTS	53
A YOUNG LONGHORN BULL	*To face* 60
SOUTH DOWN COW	,, 78
MALE AND FEMALE GAPE WORMS	84

The Vet. Book

	Page
CHICKEN GAPES	85
A TYPICAL ST BERNARD . . .	To face 94
SECTION OF HORSE'S FOOT	99
ADULT LIVER FLUKE AND WATER SNAIL . .	102
KERRY COW	To face 104
SHEEP SCAB MITE	106
SHEEP SCAB	107
A TAMWORTH SOW	To face 120
STRANGLES	129
DEVONSHIRE LONG WOOL EWES . .	To face 130
DEVON LONG WOOL RAM . . .	,, 134
WILD WHITE CATTLE	,, 136

Introduction to the Study of Disease

IN order to have a correct understanding of the elements of disease, it is expedient for the amateur to make himself acquainted with the conditions of health, which can only be done by cultivating the power of observation, together with a just appreciation of the various habits and laws governing the functional powers of the various organs, the regulation of which forms the fundamental principles not only in health, but in any departure from the same, *i.e.*, disease. The study of the healthy functions of the body is embraced within the title of physiology, and that of disease, under the term pathology, whilst the symptoms and signs presented to the mind of the observer are known as the so-called clinical features, though such features are not necessarily indicative of any particular disease, but when they are, are spoken of as pathognomonic; thus, for instance, an excessive secretion of urine is positive evidence of the existence of diabetes, and the passage of red urine, in cattle and sheep, has the same significance, though indicative of another malady, *i.e.* red water. The same remark is equally applicable to ulceration of the nasal membrane in Glanders, and numerous other instances might be given. The causation of disease is spoken of as its ætiology, and the differential characters of closely-allied maladies comes under the title of differential diagnosis.

The term enzöotic is applied to disease affecting a number of animals within a limited area, whereas epizöotic-diseases are spread over a much wider area, thus, for instance, influenza frequently assumes both these characters, whilst swine fever may exist either as an enzöotic or as an epizöotic. The most serious epizootics, affecting animals, have ceased to exist in this country. These were murrain (or cattle plague), contagious pleuro-pneumonia and foot and mouth disease; and, if it were not for the stringent legislative measures adopted against the importation of foreign cattle into this country, agriculturalists would soon suffer by the re-importation of these diseases, which are constantly present in such countries as Russia, Germany, etc. The meaning of the terms infection and contagion must be clearly understood. An infective disease is one that may be communicated, directly or indirectly, from one animal to another, either belonging to the same or to a different species. The method of infection varies. It may be that the poison is distributed through the air. If so, it is spoken of as volatile; whereas, if incapable of distribution in this manner, it is known as fixed, and a medium for its transference is through some agent—animate or inanimate; for instance, the virus may be conveyed by the clothing of man or animal; through sponges; drinking water; food; feeding-troughs; stable appliances, such as brushes, etc. Such transference may be direct or indirect. When the virus is swallowed it belongs to the former category; but when implanted into the system, by some mechanical means, it constitutes indirect transference. The term infective is preferable to the usage of contagion, because it implies all methods of the transference of disease, whereas contagion ought to be limited to disease communicated by contact, not necessarily with the individual, but likewise through the medium of some agent infecting it.

Mange and Ringworm are both contagious diseases, but they are also infective. Another drawback to the use of the term contagious is found in its inapplicability to such maladies as Swine Fever, Rabies, Anthrax, Tetanus, Actionomycosis, etc., all of which are, more correctly, designated innoculable diseases—a term that at once expresses the method of transference. The foregoing distinction concerning a class of diseases, sometimes spoken of as zymotic, has been given in order that the reader may be in a position to correctly appreciate the differences between the multifarious specific ailments he may come across affecting animals, or more correctly the channels by which they are distributed.

The different species of domestic animals behave, when labouring under diseases, in divers manners;

thus, an ox, when affected with some chest complaint, commonly assumes the recumbent attitude, whereas the horse has a preference for the standing attitude; the dog sits upon its haunches with its fore limbs outstretched during respiratory complaints, all of which attitudes are assumed for the purposes of taking advantage of the auxiliary muscles which are brought into play when the animal is labouring under defective lung aeration. Again, a horse with fever in the feet endeavours to throw the weight of its body off its pedal extremities. It will, if the fore feet are affected, throw them as far forward as possible, whereas if the hind ones are implicated, they are thrown as far under the belly as possible. The significance of attitude in relation to disease, must not be over-estimated and has no pathognomonic significance.

THE PULSE

What is the pulse? It is a series of undulations in the wall of an artery in response to an afflux of blood from the heart, and each pulsation or beat corresponds to the contraction of the heart. This is the so called "Arterial pulse" and there should be no pulsation in the veins or capillaries, —the last-named being a sort of breakwater system interposed between the arteries and the veins. The pulse constitutes a useful aid in the diagnos-

Introduction to the Study of Disease

ing of disease, but veterinarians do not always attach a great deal of significance to it, especially in cattle, dogs, sheep, etc., because of the restless nature of these animals, and the difficulty experienced in the interpretation of the various morbid phenomena consequent upon disease. Again a large amount of practical experience is indispensable in order to appreciate the changes brought about by disease. In order to feel the pulse it is essential that the wall of the artery should have a hard background to compress the vessel-wall against, and impart sensation to the fingers, the first and second of which are usually employed. It is a popular but fallacious error to believe that the pulse can only be felt in a particular artery, and veterinary surgeons sometimes resort to very different situations of the animal's body in order to ascertain the state of the pulsations. The most convenient situation to feel the pulse of the horse is at the artery winding round the lower jaw, which can readily be felt beneath the skin by rolling the finger along the lower jaw, immediately below the cheek and slightly to the inner side. The animal must be kept perfectly still for this purpose and the tips of the index and second finger pressed lightly upon the wall of the vessels, counting each rise and fall as one beat. The number of pulsations in a given time, although of some value in the elucidation of disease, is quite secondary to the *character* of such pulsation, and this is where the difficulty for the amateur arises. The normal amount of pulsations in the horse, per minute, is from 36 to 45; but in a foal this number is doubled; in the ox about 50 per minute; the dog 70 to 80; but in the animal last-named the pulse, as an aid to the diagnosis of the disease, is of no material value; and when it is taken the artery on the inner side of the thigh (femoral) is selected. Sheep, pigs and cats afford no reasonable chances for ascertaining the pulse. The pulsations are spoken of in accordance with their character, as hard or wiry, soft, quick, slow, full, regularly intermittent, irregularly intermittent, etc., etc. It is usual to count the number of pulsations in 15 seconds and multiply that number by 4. The pulse is influenced by external surroundings as well as by disease. When the so-called serous membranes, *i.e.* the pleura, peritoneum, etc., etc. are affected with disease, the pulse is usually of a particularly hard character, becoming "apparently" softer as the disease progresses towards an unfavourable issue. In liver complaints the pulse is usually slow; and in heart diseases it is either intermittent; venous; or wiry; its variability depending upon the structures chiefly implicated. In influenza—more especially during the later stages—the pulse becomes extremely feeble. Whenever the tension in the arteries is increased, as in acute engorgement of the lungs, founder, etc., the pulsations may be raised

Introduction to the Study of Disease

to perhaps 100 per minute, and their volume small; this diminution in each pulsation being due to the rapidity of the heart's contraction, and the diminished recoil in the wall of the vessel.

THE TEMPERATURE

Internal temperature, though subject to variability through external influences, of the different animals is as follows:—

Normal

Horse	100° F. to 101°
Ox	101° F. ,, 102°
Sheep	102° F. ,, 104°
Pig	102° F. ,, 103½°
Dog, or cat	101° F. ,, 102°
Fowl	104° F.
Turkey and pigeon	109° F.

The foregoing are the normal temperatures when the animal is at rest. Exercise causes a marked increase of temperature.

The instrument employed for taking the internal temperature is known as a clinical thermometer, and those in use in Great Britian are marked on the Fahrenheit scale, and obtainable from any optician or chemist for about 2s. 6d., and every stock-owner should have one of these in his possession. A clinical thermometer consists of two portions, viz, a bulb and a stem; the first-named containing the mercury. Between the bulb and stem there is a rod or detached piece of mercury. This is the "*index*" or registering agent, and before the thermometer is used it is necessary that this should be shaken down by taking hold of the stem with the fingers and shaking the thermometer. Bring it down to about 97°. In order to ascertain the temperature of an animal, take the thermometer between the tips of the fingers and insert the bulb into the rectum or lower end of the bowel, allowing it to remain in this situation for a couple of minutes or thereabouts, depending upon the time required for registration. If a horse, raise the tail with the left hand; have a man to pick up one of the fore limbs, moisten the bulb of the thermometer with spittle and insert as indicated, taking care to still retain a grasp of it whilst in its position. The clinical thermometer is one of the most valuable aids—not only for marking the rise and fall of disease, but what is of still greater importance, it affords reliable evidence during the incubative period. Slight fever is present when the temperature ranges between 102° and 104° in the horse, ox, and dog. A moderate amount of fever at 105°. High fever, at $105\frac{1}{2}$° to 107° and, an extreme fever 107° to 108°; the last named condition being intolerable for any length of time.

Very common temperatures in the horse are 105° and 106°. The same remark is equally

Introduction to the Study of Disease

applicable to the dog. The temperatures should be taken about the same hours night and morning, the evening temperature being normally slightly higher. The influence of drugs on the regulation of the bodily heat, though not affording control of febrile conditions, do unquestionably assist in diminishing the excessive oxidation of the body, which is largely influenced by its nervous mechanism. Fevers are not curable, but can be directed towards a favourable issue by acting upon the excretory organs with various medicinal agents. For instance, the bowels may be roused to activity by some saline, such as Epsom salts; the kidneys with a diuretic agent such as nitrate of potash (salt petre); whilst the activity of the skin may be markedly increased either by clothing the body with woollen rugs, or through the administration of a diaphoretic drug, the secretion of sweat assisting to unload the economy of its deleterious products.

THE RESPIRATIONS

The respiratory movements are liable to considerable variations, not only in health but also in disease, and the variability of such movements is sometimes increased proportionately to the pulsations. Age, sex, temperament, exercise, and external surroundings in general, have a marked influence over the respiratory movements, whilst the influence of drugs and disease acts in a similar manner. The normal number of respirations in a horse is, approximately, from 12 to 16 per minute, but in disease, likewise after exercise, this number may be multiplied four or five times. The value of the respiratory movements as an aid to the diagnosis of disease is not of very great importance, but as a general statement it is fairly accurate to say that diseases of the lungs are characterised by accelerated breathing, but in pleurisy the movements are slow and painful, the inspiratory movements being performed with difficulty, through the pain induced by this act. In addition to what is called thoracic breathing, there is in the complaint last alluded to the so-called abdominal breathing, which implies the usage of the auxiliary muscles of respiration. The mere fact of an animal having accelerated breathing does not necessarily imply defective respiratory power. On the other hand it is significant, though for a correct interpretation of such significance there are many difficulties confronting the amateur.

There is a diseased condition known as emphysema of the lungs or broken wind, in which the respiratory movements are pathognomonic, and will be referred to under their respective headings.

Mucous Membranes

The visible mucous membranes, *i.e.*, those lining the eyelids, mouth and nose, and likewise the

Introduction to the Study of Disease

external generative organs in the female, are frequently referred to by veterinary surgeons for the purpose of ascertaining the degree of vascular disturbance existing within the body.

In bloodless conditions of the body the membranes are pale, whereas in inflammatory states they are considerably heightened in colour, and the minute vessels ramifying over the surface and entering into their structure show marked injection, *i.e*, they appear to be distended. In a class of diseases, chiefly of a specific nature, the mucous membranes are studded with minute blood-spots indicative of a vitiated condition of the blood. All these membranes express outwardly, a similar state of the mucous membranes within the body, and in liver complaints the jaundiced colour of these membranes shows that the liver is not performing its functions properly.

Age and Sex

Both of these exert an influence in the production of disease, likewise in the ultimate issue. Old animals are predisposed to become afflicted with diseases of the eye; of the bones and joints; of the teeth; and diseases of senility. On the other hand young animals alone suffer from such complaints as joint-ill and inflammation of the umbilical cord; from acute scour, and (with exceptions) such diseases as Strangles, Canine Distemper, etc., etc.

The Vet. Book

Females are liable to complaints from which the male is exempt, to say nothing of the multifarious ailments arising through foaling, calving, lambing, whelping, etc.

The reparative power of the aged is necessarily much less than that of the young, and in no cases is this more typically exemplified than in fractures and wounds.

What has been said with reference to the female, is equally applicable, though conversely, to the male, the generative apparatus of which is very liable to be the seat of various morbid processes.

Surroundings

The conditions under which an animal is living, not only have an influence in determining the onset of disease but exert a power in the ultimate issue; thus, for instance, if an animal is badly housed or badly fed, or mismanaged in some other way, and disease makes its appearance, the chances are that a severe form of the malady will be assumed, or unfavourable complications arise.

The environment of an animal very often leads to the immediate production of disease or, it may be, death. This is exemplified in the case of animals pastured, or allowed to graze where poisonous herbage exists; and the plants which commonly play a part are the Yew; Fox Glove; the Deadly Nightshade; the Rhododendron; the Bitter-sweet; the Henbane; the Lilac; the Laburnum; the

Introduction to the Study of Disease

Bryony, etc., etc. Hence the necessity for the complete exclusion and extermination of such herbage from grazing ground.

Attention to thorough cleanliness of stables, cow-houses, piggeries, poultry-houses, and kennels, etc., etc., constitute the main principles for the guidance, and regulation, not only of health, but also of disease.

Heredity

Under the title of heredity must be included a class of diseases which from time immemorial have been looked upon as capable of being handed from parent to progeny, either directly or indirectly. Some diseases are apparently transmitted either from Sire or Dam to their offspring; whereas, in other cases, several generations may elapse before the development of the malady. To this the term Atavism is applied, which really means "harking back." It is well known that many of these so-called "hereditary" diseases are not derived from the parent, but are the outcome of causes operating extrinsically, and bear no relationship to hereditary predisposition. Peculiarity of conformation does unquestionably play an active part in determining disease, and this constitutes one of the chief factors of hereditary predisposition; for instance, a horse that has over-bent or sickle-shaped hocks, is more liable " to spring a curb,' than one with good hock conformation; whilst hocks that are narrow below, or "tied in," favour the development of bone spavin. Heredity shows itself quite apart from disease and constitutes the basis of selection, or the production of pedigree stock. The direct transference of disease from parent to progeny (Congenital disease) most certainly does exist and Tuberculosis has been found in animals immediately they are born, but such is quite exceptional.

Such disease as Tuberculosis has always been looked upon as of a strictly hereditary nature, but since, the recognition of the specific organisms and their almost constant presence in vitiated surroundings has, to a large extent, modified these views. The presence of disease in a fœtus "in utero," is the best proof of its hereditary nature.

Acquired disease is that which arises subsequent to birth, as opposed to that of a hereditary nature.

Specific or Germ Diseases

This term is applied to a class of diseases arising from special causes and mostly due to parasites, either of vegetable or animal origin. Some diseases, such as Red-water in cattle, arise through a class of minute organisms known as protozoa, and the organisms which produce this disease are introduced into the blood of cattle through the cattle Tick. They are of exceedingly minute size and exist within the white blood cells, as elongated bodies with whip-like extremities, but in order to

Introduction to the Study of Disease

detect them, it is necessary to resort to microscopic examination, for which professional aid is required. They are known as flagellated infusoria, and many other diseases in tropical countries arise from a similar cause. Internal parasites, such as worms, are known as entozoa, in contra-distinction to animal parasites residing on the outside of the body and which are termed epizoa. Round and flat worms afford a good example of the former class, and mange mites of the latter.

The detrimental influences of the entozoa is due to their mode of life, their nourishment being directly derived from their host, and in some cases their destructive effects upon the living tissues. Epizoa, on the other hand, excite congestion of the skin and live upon, and multiply within the products of the inflamed area. Ringworm is a very common disease in calves and results from invasion of the hair and hair follicles by a vegetable fungus belonging to a class of parasites known as Protophyta, which are allied to the yeast plant. Diseases, such as Anthrax, Tuberculosis, Glanders, Swine Fever, Distemper, Strangles, Influenza, etc., are due to a class of microscopic organisms known as Bacteria, Bacilli, Micro-cocci, etc., all of which are capable of marvellous powers of multiplication, requiring high powers of the microscope for their demonstration, along with suitable staining re-agents,

They belong to the Protophyta and can be cultivated on suitable media outside the body. They are divided into disease-producing and non-disease-producing classes, and some require oxygen for their growth, whilst others its complete exclusion. For instance, the germs of anthrax, when circulating in the blood of the living animal, exist in the form of minute rods, and these rods, in order to multiply, divide transversely, but directly the blood is exposed to the air, the organisms form long chains of spores as a method of multiplication, and these spores have remarkable powers of vitality; hence the reason why an anthrax grave may constitute a source of infection for an indefinite period. A singular feature in connection with the germs of anthrax is their immediate destruction by the organisms of putrefaction, and this is one reason why the germs of anthrax are so frequently absent from the blood. Some organisms are capable of distribution through the air, the germs of Tuberculosis forming a good example, and this is spoken of as a volatile poison. The methods of multiplication are usually of a very simple character—the parent organism usually dividing and sub-dividing. The destruction of germs is, as a rule, easier than that of their spores, but there are agents capable of destroying both, provided that a sufficient length of time is allowed. Extremes of heat and cold—more especially the former—usually act adversely upon them, but

Introduction to the Study of Disease

are not necessarily destructive. Such agents as formalin, chinosol, corrosive sublimate, carbolic acid, and chlorine gas, etc., will destroy most organisms and their spores, hence the advisibility for the employment of one of these agents in the cleansing of places where these diseases have been. The free admission of sunlight and pure air are potent factors in the destruction of micro-organisms; and should never be excluded from the stable, cow-house, kennels, etc., etc. All specific diseases are capable of being carried through a multiplicity of channels, such as clothing, hands, feeding and grooming appliances, through the drinking water and food; by rodents, such as rats, mice, rabbits, and hares, etc., as well as by flies, birds and insects in general. This is one of the reasons why the spontaneity of disease has been and still is, persisted in by those ignorant of the methods of dissemination.

INFLUENCE OF SOIL, CLIMATE, ETC.

Locality has a most important influence in determining the presence or absence of certain diseases, and it may be taken as a general rule that upland pastures are much freer from disease than the lowlands. Taking a couple of examples familiar to all sheep raisers, we have only to mention foot-rot and liver-rot. The prevalence of these maladies on low-lying marshy soil is too well known to be open to doubt, whilst a humid soil, more especially when there is a moist warm temperature prevailing, constitutes a predisposing factor in determining the existence of anthrax, providing there be a source of infection present, such as an anthrax grave or a decomposing anthrax carcase. Cape-horse sickness is most prevalent during the rainy seasons and before the sun has taken the dew off the grass. All diseases of a parasitic nature are favoured by the presence of moisture and warmth; frosty weather constituting a natural method of curtailing the spread of most specific diseases of man and animals, though by no means absolutely destructive of such. A clay or retentive soil is one which rather favours disease, whilst a sandy or gravelly soil confers some measure of immunity. Drainage of land may be either natural or artificial, but is essential where animals are allowed to graze. The pollution of streams by sewage water—more especially that from mills, employing chemicals in the manufacture of their goods—generally exerts a very detrimental influence upon stock drinking therefrom, whilst the careless distribution of material from painters' pots frequently leads to the destruction of cattle. The same remark is equally applicable to grazing horses and cattle in the neighbourhood of lead smelting works, where both acute and chronic forms of lead poisoning occur. The careless distribution of sheep dipping

Introduction to the Study of Disease

water and weed killers are sometimes an occasional cause of death.

Spring and autumn usually produce a large percentage of cases, Influenza, Strangles, and Distemper, whilst Red-water in young stock is most prevalent in the autumn. When land has been fouled by disease, such as Black-Quarter, it will be liable to perpetuate this malady, unless it has been dressed with lime, salt, or ploughed. The same remark applies to poultry-runs and pheasantries where such diseases as Roup, Enteric, Gapes, etc. have been; and every poultry breeder and game-farmer is well acquainted with the truth of this statement.

The VET. BOOK

Chapter I.—Anatomical Rudiments of Domestic Animals

IN this chapter the Author intends to give a brief survey of some of the elementary anatomical facts appertaining to various domesticated animals, believing that even a trifling amount of knowledge concerning such will be of interest and service, enabling the reader to have a better understanding concerning the various internal organs, joints, bones, etc., thus facilitating the diagnosis of disease.

The Horse

The term endo-skeleton is applied to that of a horse, because it is clothed externally by flesh or muscle, and encloses the body cavity. It is composed of a number of bony segments, most of which exist in pairs. The Head consists of numerous bones, mostly of a flat character, united together by sutures, and these lines are plainly marked in the young animal, gradually undergoing obliteration in the later years. The cranial cavity is divided

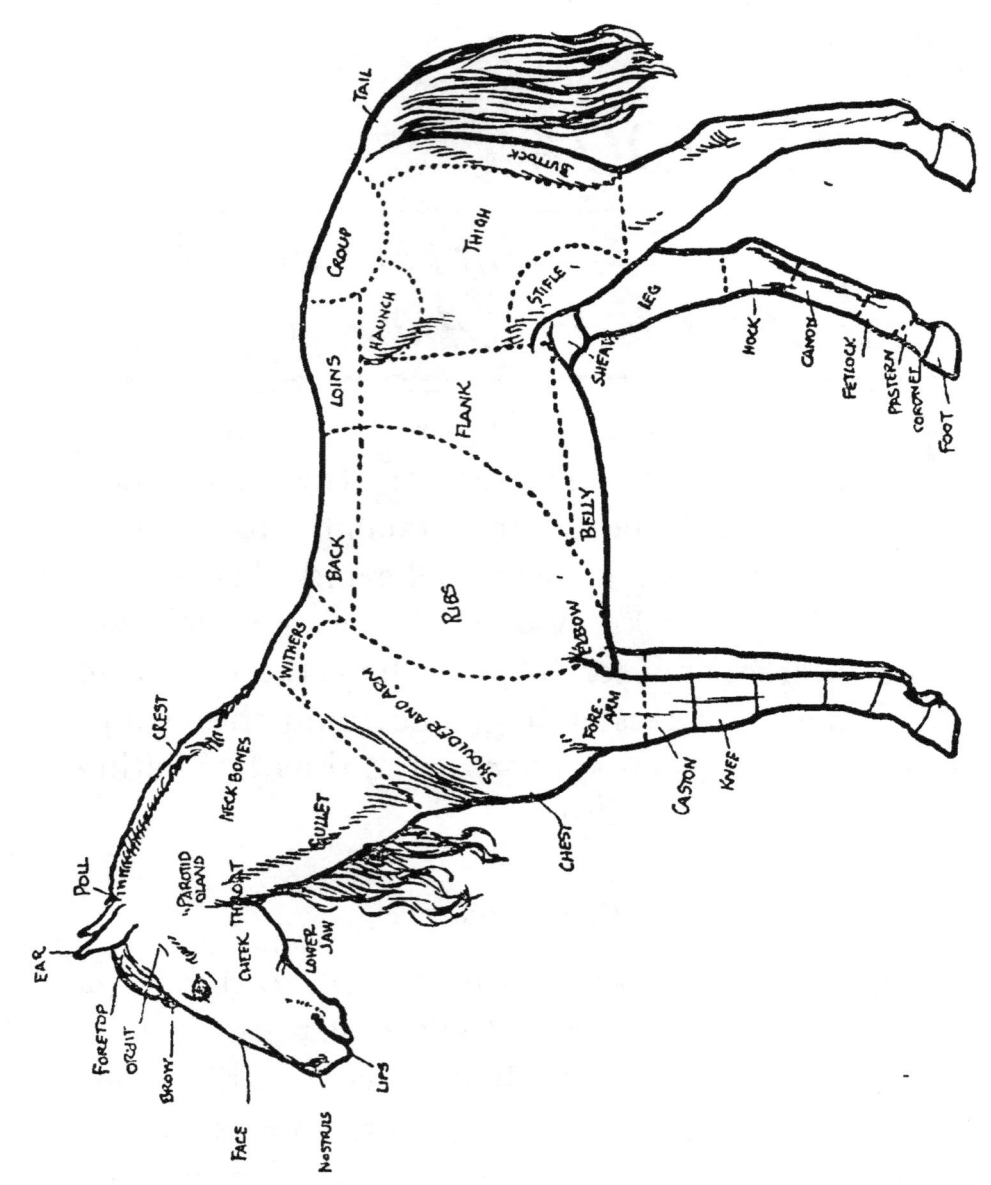

THE EXTERIOR OF THE HORSE

Anatomical Rudiments

into two compartments, and encloses the brain. The cavities for the eyes are complete. The lower jaws are strong and in each jaw there are six molar teeth—upper and lower (24 in all). Twelve of these are temporary—three in each jaw and known as the 1st, 2nd and 3rd molars, whilst the 4th, 5th and 6th are permanent. In addition to the molar teeth there are six incisors in the upper and six in the lower jaw, all of which are temporary and are entirely replaced as soon as the animal has turned $4\frac{1}{4}$ years. These teeth come up in pairs at intervals of a year and are known as the centrals; laterals; and corners; in accordance with their position. The first pair, or centrals, make their appearance soon after the animal has turned 2 years and are about half way up at $2\frac{1}{2}$ years, meeting each other at 3 years. The laterals appear at $3\frac{1}{4}$ years and the corners at $4\frac{1}{4}$ years or thereabout, being later in animals in the North. The neck is composed of 7 bones. The back and the loins of 21 vertebrae and the sacrum of about 5 segments, whilst the tail has numerous small bones. There is no collar bone as in man, and the forelimbs are not attached to the skeleton but are suspended by muscles. The hind limbs, on the other hand, are united to the skeleton, by the pelvic girdle or basin-bone, which, in reality, is composed of three segments on each side. Each hind limb consists of a femur (or thigh bone) which is the largest bone in the body and articulates

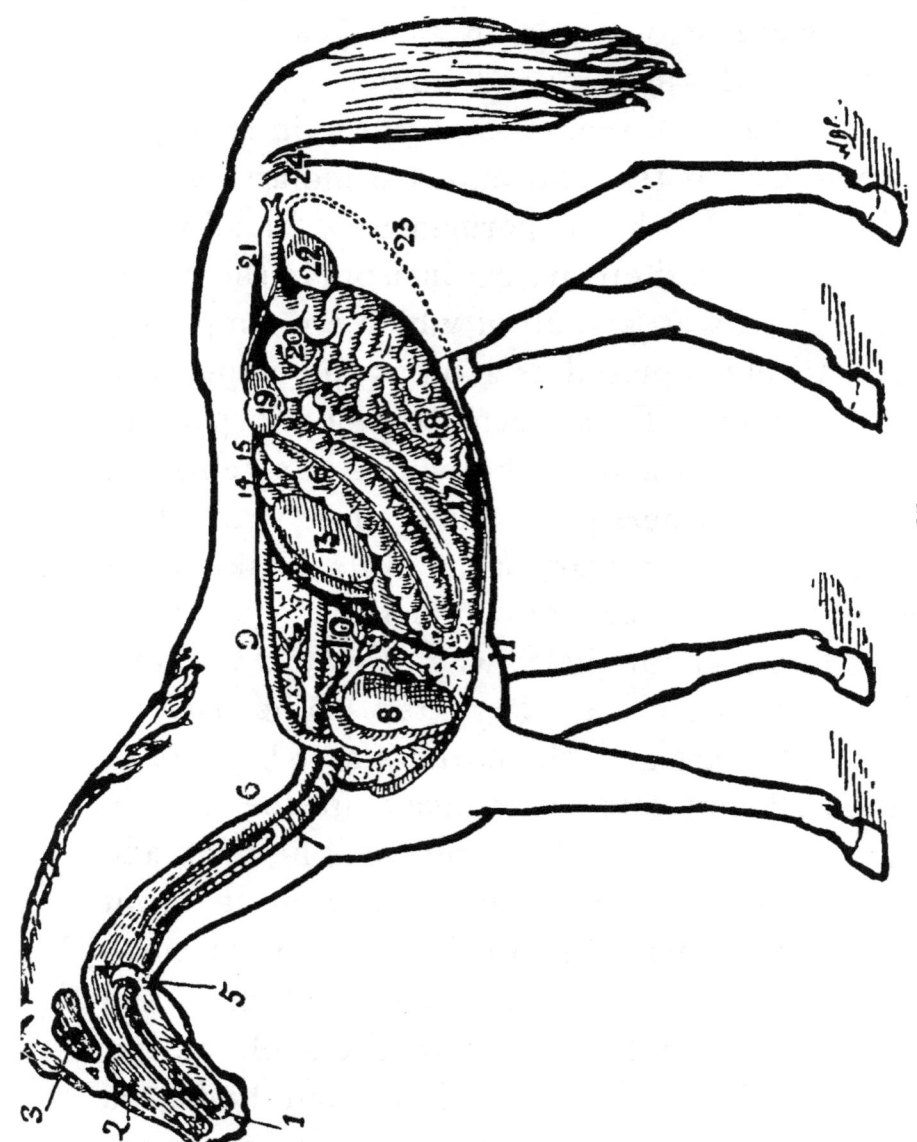

PARTS OF THE HORSE

1, Mouth; 2, nasal cavity; 3, cranial cavity; 4, pharynx; 5, epiglottis; 6, œsophagus, or gullet; 7, windpipe; 8, heart; 9, the great abdominal artery; 10, lungs; 11, diaphragm; 12, spleen; 13, stomach; 14, arterial branches to supply viscera; 15, liver; 16, the great colon; 17, cæcum; 18, small intestines; 19, left kidney; 20, floating intestine; 21, rectum; 22, bladder; 23, urethra; 24, anus.

Anatomical Rudiments

below with a second thigh (or tibia) and also with the patella or knee-cap. Interposed between these two thigh bones is a pair of cartilaginous discs. The rest of the limb corresponds to that of the fore-limbs. The fore-limbs have greater bodily weight to bear than the hind ones, and it may be accepted as a general statement that these show evidences of wear quicker than the hind ones. The fore-limb is composed of the scapula (or shoulder blade) which is articulated to the humerus (or arm) by a ball and socket joint, and the arm, in its turn, articulates with the radius by a hinge joint. The lower end of the radius rests upon the upper row of the carpal bones, of which there are 7 or 8 in the horse, corresponding to the wrist in man. Below the carpus is the large metacarpal (or cannon) bone, and articulated with the back of it, are two slender rods of bones—the small metacarpals—and the lower end of the large cannon bone, forms a hinge with the first phalanx, which is followed by the second phalanx; and then the third phalanx or coffin bone; the two last-named being embedded within the hoof. In addition to this, at the articulation *between* the cannon and the phalanx, are two small pyramidal-shaped bones, known as the "*sesamoids*," whilst at the back of the pedal articulation, there is a little bone known as the navicular which is often the seat of disease. There are 18 pairs of ribs, 8 of which are true and 10 false. The 8 true ribs join the 8 segments of the breast bone. The respiratory organs are well developed, and com-

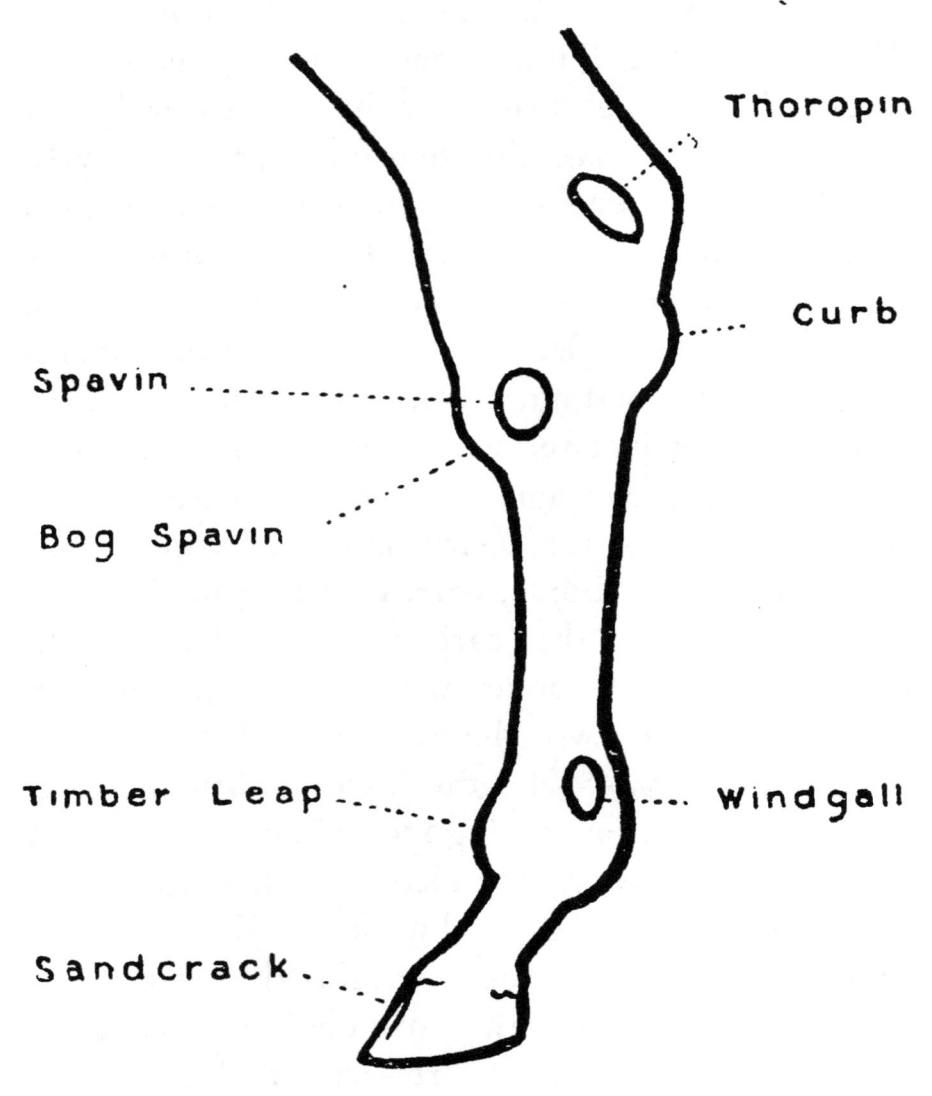

SEATS OF DISEASES OF HORSE'S HIND-LEG

prise the nasal cavities, the larynx, the trachea, the bronchial tubes and lungs. The heart is large and is divided into four chambers, the blood vessels are large and have strong thick walls.

Anatomical Rudiments

The tongue is small as compared with that of the ox. The gullet begins at the pharynx and has, on each side of it, a pouch. These are the gutteral pouches. The gullet is long, but has a very small opening into the stomach, and enters the latter in a peculiar manner. The stomach is composed of 3 coats and is small, having a capacity of between 3 and 4 gallons, but the small size of this organ is compensated for by the large size and capacity of the intestines, which are divided into large and small portions. The small gut begins at the outlet of the stomach and ends in the blind gut or cæcum, its entrance into which is guarded by a valve. The large gut comprises the cæcum, the double colon, the single or floating colon, and the rectum or straight gut. The total capacity of the large gut is about 20 gallons, and the small one 12 gallons.

The liver is large and its chief function is to secrete bile and act as a storehouse for starch. The spleen (or milt) is about $3\frac{1}{2}$ lbs. weight and is attached to the stomach. The pancreas (or sweetbread) is one of the principal organs concerned in digestion. The thoracic-duct is a large absorbent vessel situated in the chest and begins under the loins. The kidneys are large and situated beneath the loins. They secrete the urine, from which it passes by the ureters to the bladder, and from the latter by the urethra to without. The female generative organs com-

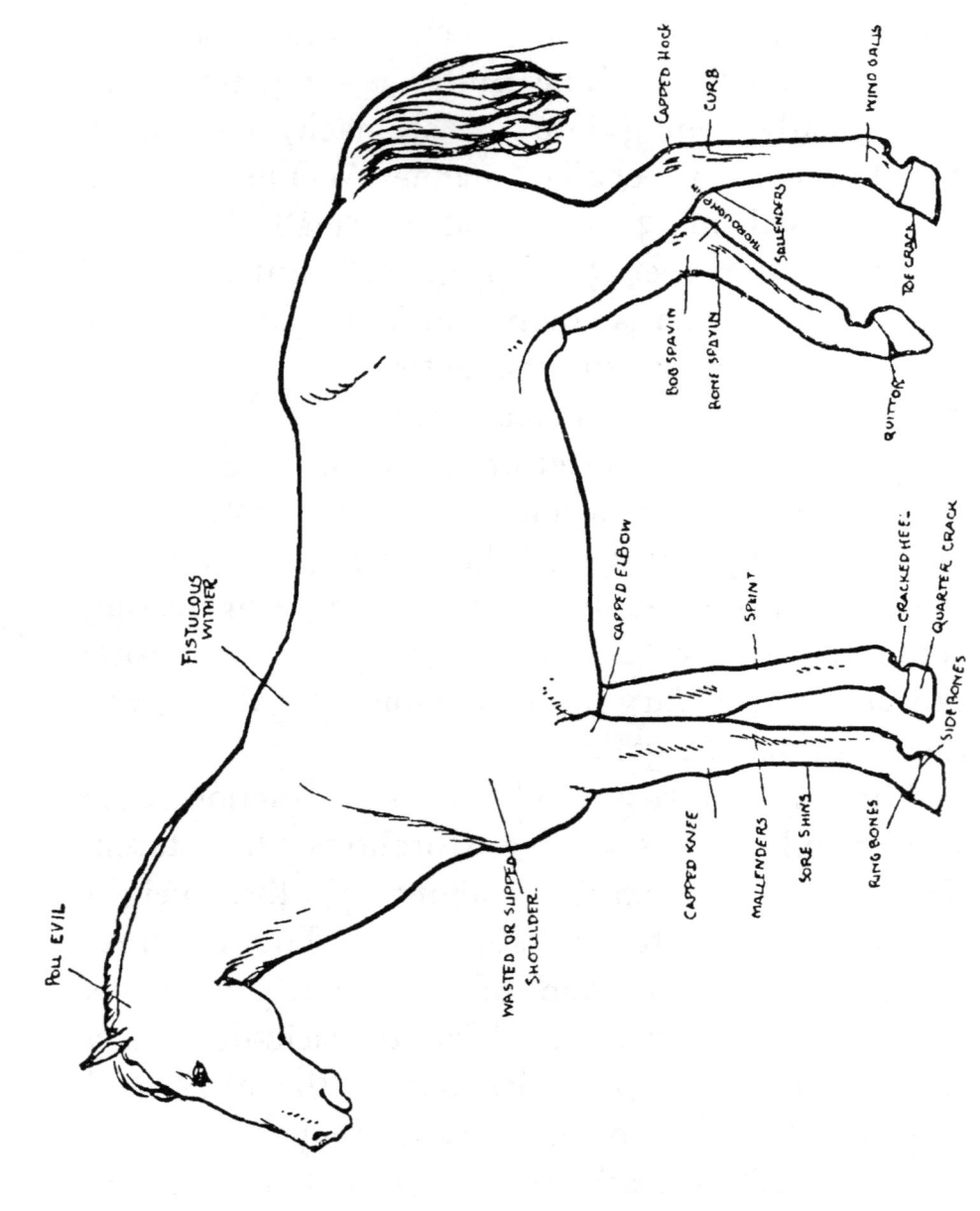

Seats of Diseases in the Horse

prise the ovaries; their ducts; the uterus; the vagina; the vulva; and the mammary gland. The male organs are the testes; their ducts; the seminal reservoirs; the generative organ, etc.

The nervous system is well developed, and comprises the brain and spinal cord. There are 12 pairs of nerves which take origin from both these structures. The distribution of the nerves (divided into sensory and motor) enables the animal to experience the various sensations throughout its body, and execute its movements.

The muscular system obtains its maximum development in the horse and upon the excellency of this, beauty of conformation largely depends. The muscles clothing the back and the loins are the largest in the body. They mostly exist in pairs and there are no muscles below the knees or hocks—nothing beyond their tendinous prolongations. The flexor muscles are situated at the back of the limbs and the extensors in front. Every muscle has its point of origin and insertion in some bone, excepting the so-called sphincters, which have neither origin nor insertion. The muscles encircling the anus, and the pupils of the eye form good examples. The contraction of muscle can be produced by artificial stimulation, but under ordinary circumstances such contraction is induced by motor nerves. The first muscle under the skin almost covers the entire body and is the one that enables the animal to shake irritating foreign substances off its skin.

The hair (or coat) is shed in the spring and

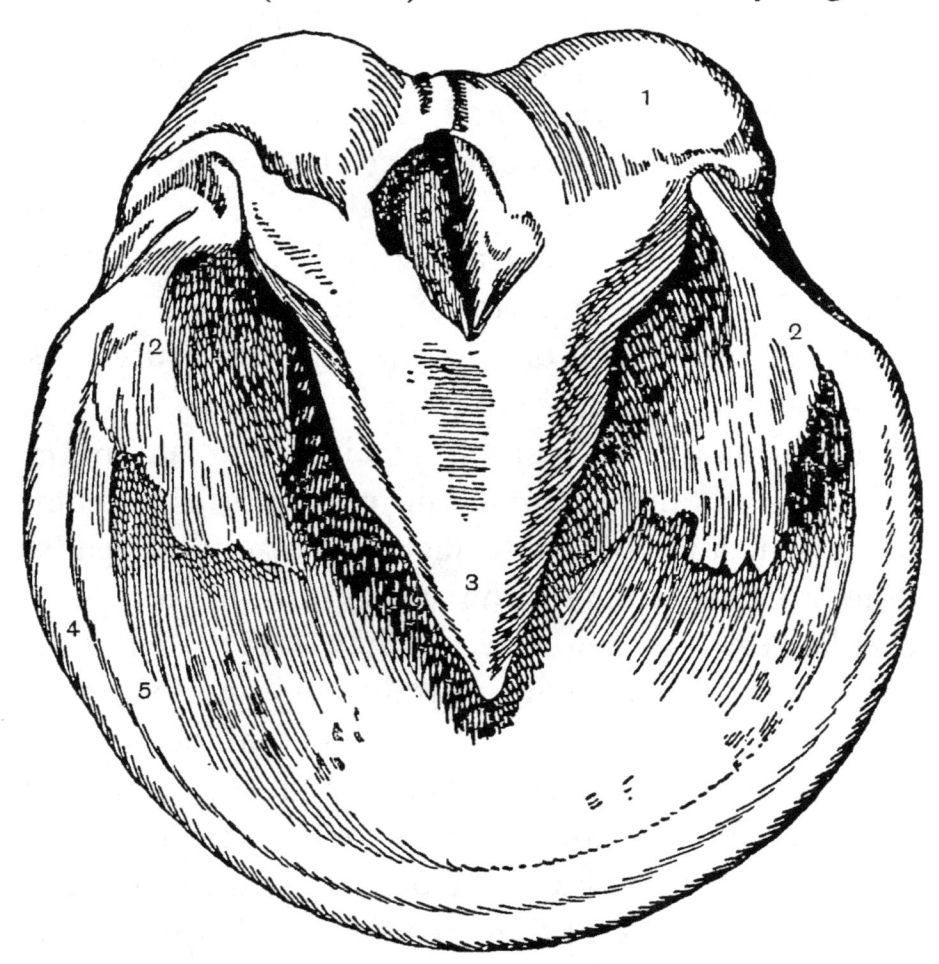

GROUND SURFACE OF HORSE'S FOOT
1, heels; 2, bars; 3, frog; 4, wall; 5, white line.

autumn, except in that of the mane and tail which is permanent. There are both sweat glands and sebaceous glands in the skin, but the former are practically absent from the limbs.

The hoof is a modified epidermal structure

Anatomical Rudiments

and encircled by a band round its upper portion. This is the coronary band, and the hoof-wall is secreted by papillæ on this structure. The hoof is divided into a toe portion; quarters; and heels; and on its lower surface is the horny sole with a triangular pad of elastic tissue, known as the *frog*. On either side of the frog are the bars—reflections of the wall, and it is important that neither the frog, or bars should ever be pared by the shoeing-smith. The inner surface of the hoof is studded over with numerous leaf-life projections, known as the *insensitive* laminæ, which are dove-tailed into corresponding fleshy ones on the wall of the pedal bone, and are termed sensitive laminæ. The lower surface of the pedal bone is arched, and covered by a vascular membrane known as the sensitive sole. The backward prolongations of the pedal bone comprise two flexible plates of cartilage. These are the lateral cartilages, so commonly the seat of disease in heavy horses. The foot has a rich blood supply, but the veins have no valves.

THE OX, SHEEP AND GOAT

The skeleton of the ox, though differing in certain minor respects, is practically identical with that of the horse, but the individual bones are relatively heavier—not being an animal of swift progression. In the upper jaw there are no incisor teeth, these being replaced by a pad of

Heart and Stomach of the Ox

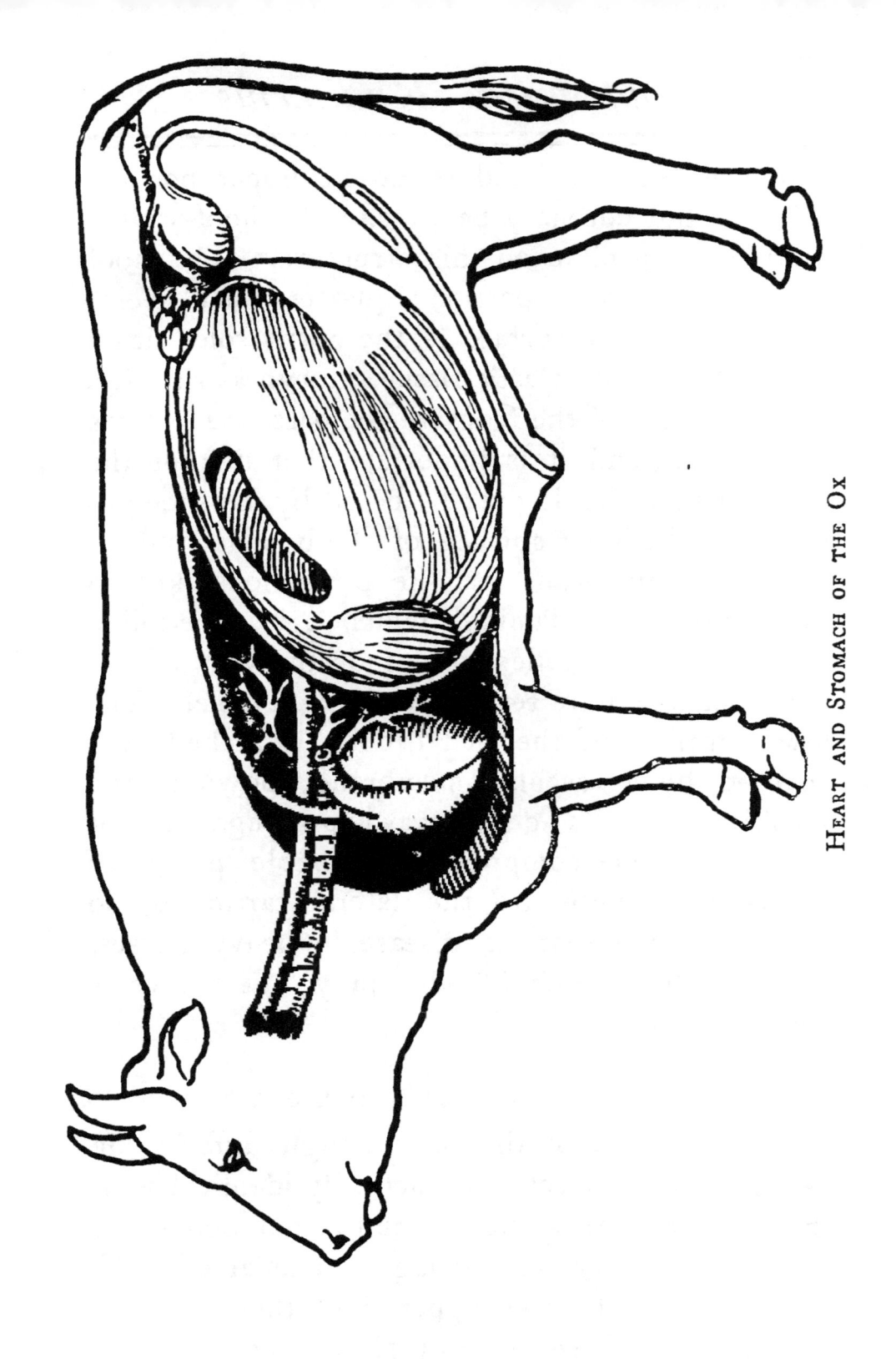

Anatomical Rudiments

fibrous tissue. There are 8 incisors in the lower jaw, and an interesting feature in connection with these is that they are loose in their sockets. The stomachs of all ruminants are divided into 4 compartments, and the names of these are as follows: the Rumen (paunch) or 1st compartment; the Reticulum (honey-comb) or 2nd compartment; the Omasum (Manyplies) or 3rd compartment; the Abomasum (4th compartment) or true digestive stomach; the last named being, in the calf, the largest; and contains a substance called rennet, used in the manufacture of cheese. The capacity of the ox's stomach is enormous but that of the intestines small. The ox, sheep and goat all chew their cud; the food passing, first of all into the paunch, but after its regurgitation into the mouth to be chewed, it passes into the 2nd compartment, whilst the juices are extracted from it in the 3rd compartment, the lining of which is specially adapted for this purpose; subsequently finding its way into the 4th compartment where true digestion begins. The gullet in ruminants is wide. The lungs of the ox have a large amount of connective tissue, and this is favourable to the grapy-like growths so commonly observed in tuberculosis. The kidneys are lobulated and large; but in sheep and goats, are like those of the dog, pig, etc., viz. simple. The liver is large and has a gall bladder, which latter is absent in the horse. In the calf there is a so-called thymus gland situated at the

The Exterior of the Cow.

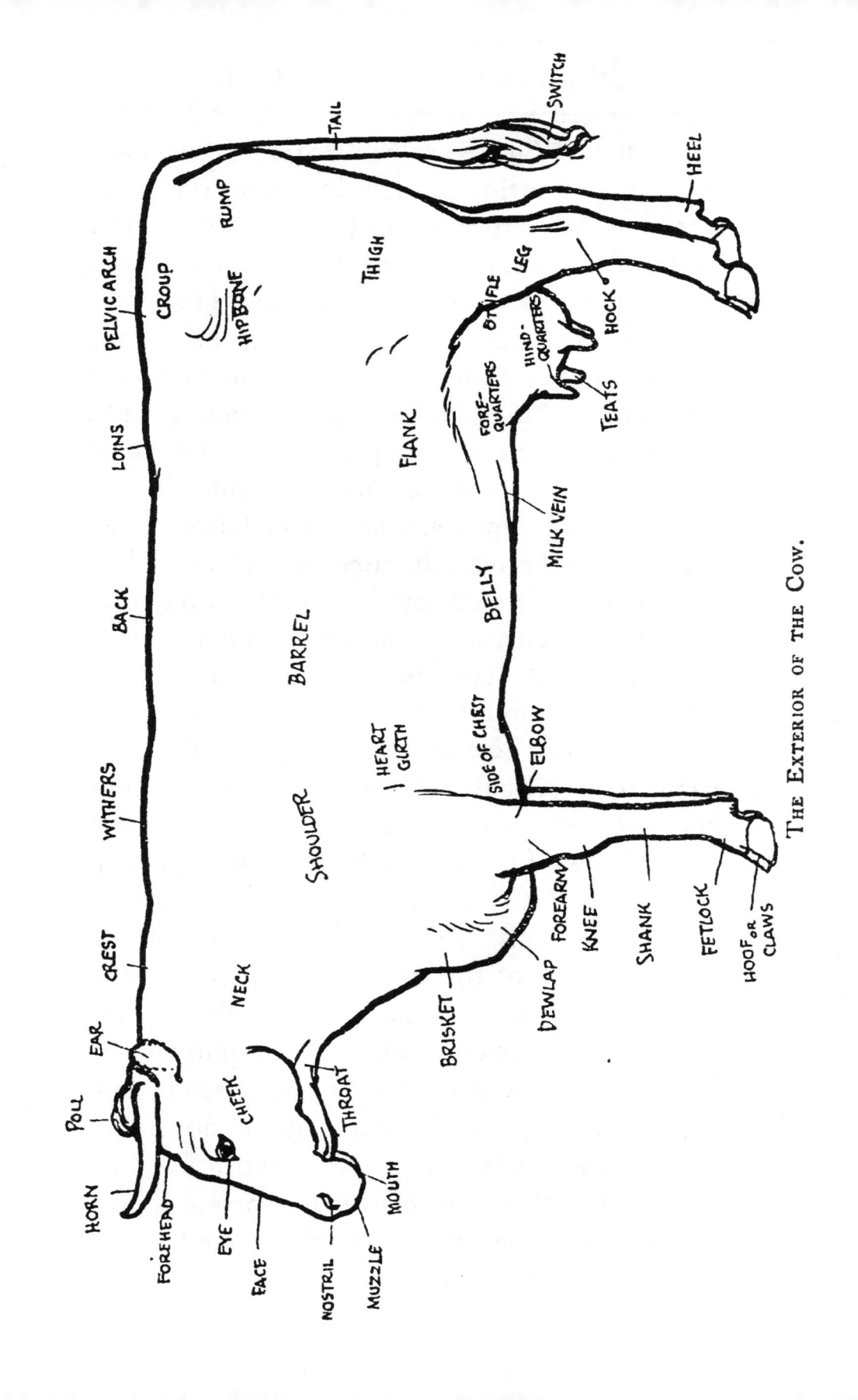

PARTS OF THE OX

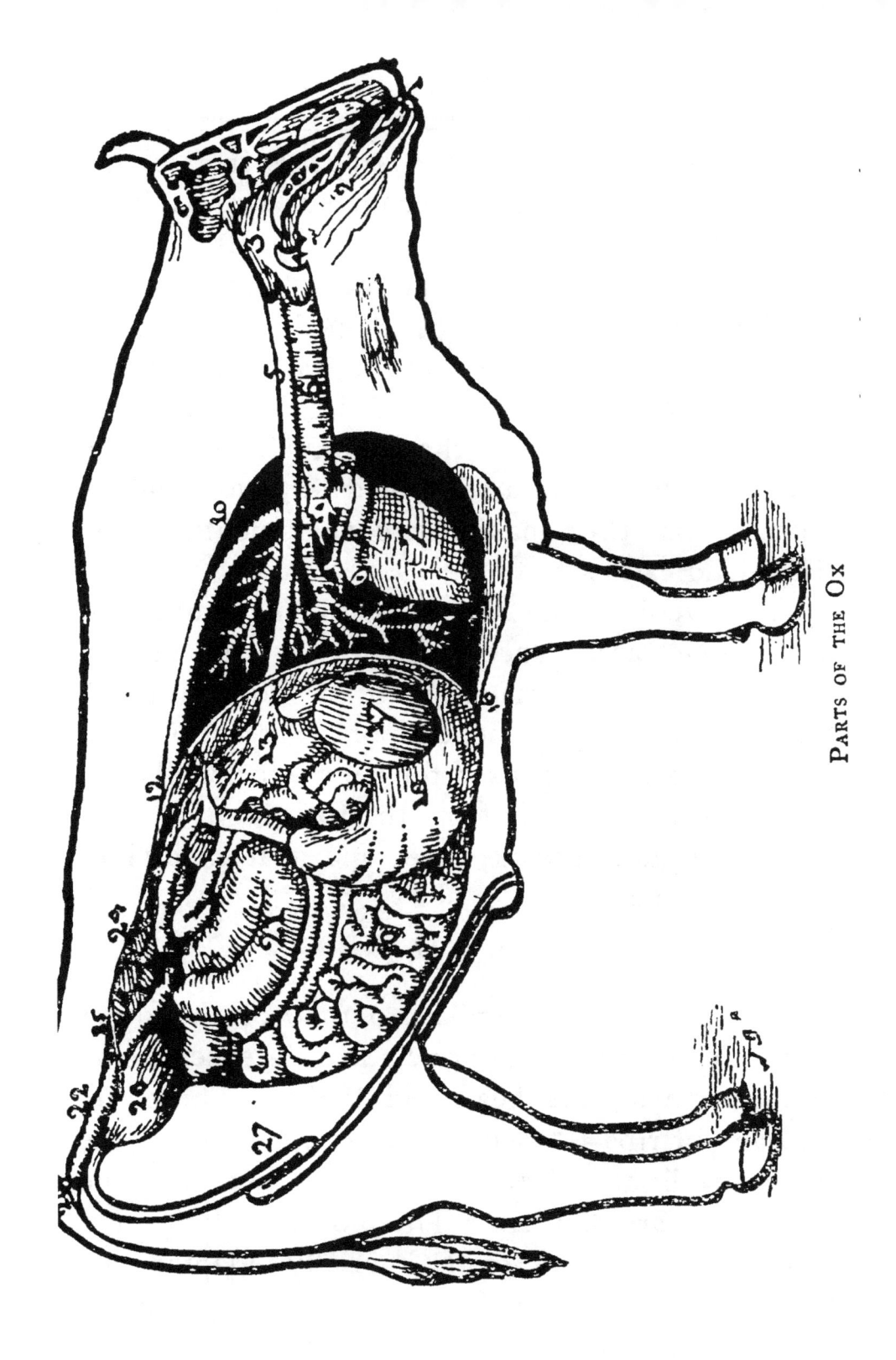

root of the neck, but this disappears in later life. The spleen (or milt) is elongated and, as in all other animals, is enclosed in a capsule. In the female, the urethra is short and straight, whereas in the male it takes an S shaped curve, which precludes the passage of the catheter, by the ordinary method. The skin is thick, and less sensitive than that of the horse. The eyes are placed so as to give a wide field of vision, and the horns obtain their maximum development in West Highland cattle.

The wool of the sheep varies in quantity and texture in accordance with the breeds, and its application in the manufacture of woollen goods depends upon its fineness, or coarseness; the coarser wools being used for rugs, etc., whilst the finer fabrics are made from the former.

The digits in the ox, sheep and goat are divided (cloven foot).

The Pig

The skeleton is similar to that of the other domestic animals, the principal differences being connected with the head and limbs. There are 14 pairs of ribs—7 being true and 7 false. The bones are light and porous, and the feet, as in the ruminants, are divided. The mouth is large and capacious, and the teeth specially adapted for tearing, and the snout for digging. The stomach is simple and the gullet wide. The teats of the sow are arranged in two parallel lines, extending from the abdominal to the sternal region. Gestation is multiparous. The pig is omnivorous, and as an aid to digestion a liberal supply of coal should be allowed, apparently proving beneficial.

The Dog and the Cat

The skeletons of both are particularly adapted for rapid progression and the muscular system is well developed; the olfactory bulbs, or organs of smell, are large and the sense of smell keen. The brain attains only a moderate degree of development, much less than that of the monkey or parrot. The molar teeth are specially adapted for flesh-tearing and 4 tushes are present. The muscles of mastication are large and there is a deep pit to lodge the muscles of the lower jaw. The orbital arch is incomplete above in both animals—a short ligament completing the arch above. The skull varies remarkably in the different varieties of the dog, attaining its maximum length in such breeds as the Borzois and Greyhound; whilst for girth and heaviness the St Bernard and Mastiff, Great Dane, etc., are conspicuous. The lungs surround the heart, and breathing takes place both through the mouth and nose, whereas in the horse it is through the nose only. In order to keep the temperature to its normal standard, the dog pants, there being very slight perspiration through the skin. The chest cavity of the dog is large and there are 13 pairs of ribs on each side—9 true and 4 false.

The stomach is simple and the gullet wide at its entrance, which facilitates vomiting at will; whereas the outlet of it is close which prevents food from readily passing out into the bowels.

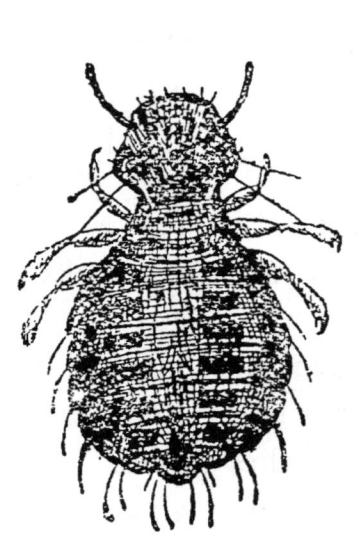

Fowl Louse
(*Goniocotes hologaster*)
(greatly enlarged)

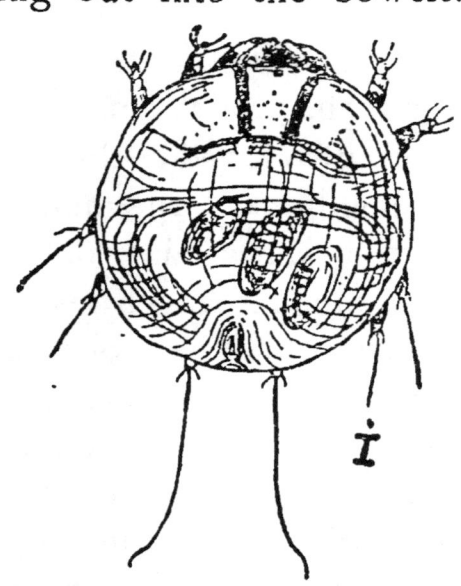

Feather-Eating or Depluming Scabies (*Sarcoptes laevis*)
Egg-bearing female (greatly enlarged)

Digestive functions are slow. As in other animals the liver is situated on the right side, behind and under cover of the last two ribs. The teats are arranged similarly to those of the pig, and the bulk of the generative apparatus is contained within the pelvic cavity. The digits are divided into four, and the distal extremity is provided with a claw, which in the cat is retractile—there

Anatomical Rudiments

being in this animal special ligaments for this purpose. In some breeds of both the dog and cat the tail is either aborted, or entirely absent.

THE FOWL

The bony framework is pneumatic, there being numerous air sacs in connection with the bones and lungs. The epidermal appendages are in the form of feathers and upon the legs there are numerous epidermal scales. There are four toes, and the bones of the hock are fused with that of the metatarsal bone. There is a rudimentary tail, and the bones of the neck are numerous and vary in accordance with the species of fowl. The breast bone

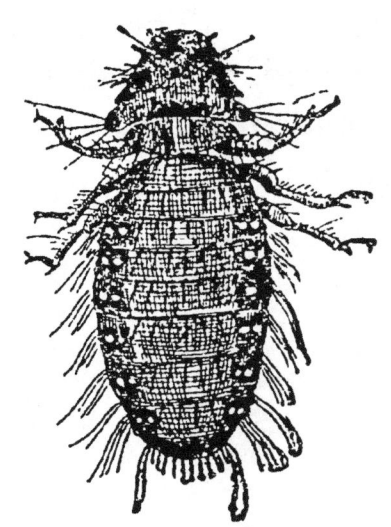

FOWL LOUSE (*Menopon pallidum*) (greatly enlarged)

has a prominent keel in birds of swift progression, but in aquatic birds is flat. There are both true and false ribs, and the shoulder blade is sword-shaped; and there is a pro-

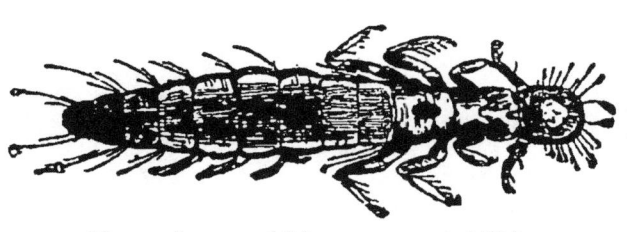

FOWL LOUSE (*Lipeurus variabilis*) (greatly enlarged)

minent bone, known as the furculum, or merrythought. The bones of the pelvis are fused, the gullet has a dilated part known as the ingluvies (or crop), which serves for the storage of grain. Immediately below this is the continuation of the digestive tube, and in all seed-eating birds there is a gizzard or muscular organ for grinding the food, but between this and the crop is the true digestive stomach. The intestines really begin with the gizzard and end at the cloaca, *i.e.*, an aperture common to the urinary, and alimentary passages.

Chapter II.—General Management in Disease

Administering Medicines

THE administration of medicine to the various animals requires a certain amount of skill and practice, and the writer has been astonished how very seldom horse-keepers, kennelmen, etc., can give an animal a dose of medicine in a proper manner. Some horses are very easily drenched, whereas others are extremely difficult to give medicine to; and in exceptional instances, it is impossible to do so.

This frequently results through previous abuse, hence the necessity of firm but careful handling during its administration.

Sheep and pigs require great care, otherwise they will be choked. Liquids should be given very slowly to both these animals, and the maximum amount of fluid for either should not, as a rule, exceed a pint. For holding the fluid an old shoe, with the toe cut out, is the best for pigs; whereas for sheep, a horn or bottle does very well. So long as a pig continues to feed, the best plan is to give medicine in combination with the food. If forcible administration is resorted to,

The Vet. Book

a noose should be put round the upper jaw and held by an assistant.

Cattle are easily drenched, and several quarts of liquid may be given, but the average amount is

DRENCHING A PIG

about a quart. A horn, tin, or glass bottle having a capacity of not less than a pint does very well, and should be grasped with the right hand, whilst the left hand is passed around the head and in at the left hand side of the jaw, so as to bring

COTSWOLD RAM

General Management in Disease

pressure on to the roof of the mouth and pull the head backwards. Cattle will often take powders in their food and such should be given mixed with damp corn, etc. For the horse, drugs may be given either in liquid or solid form, and some horses will take even very pungent drugs along with their food, whereas others refuse such in any form, when mixed with their food.

A convenient method of giving the horse medicine is in the form of an electuary, in which the active agents are combined with some sticky substance, such as treacle, etc. This method is particularly valuable in cases of sore throat, etc., and diminishes the risk of choking the patient. It can also be used for dogs. Balls are largely used for horses, but a certain amount of skill and practice is requisite. The use of a balling gun, made of leather is advisable for amateurs, and any saddler will construct such an appliance for a few shillings.

In giving liquids to the horse, the draught ought not to exceed, say, a pint, and is preferably given out of a half-pint tin-bottle. It is necessary to place the head under restraint, and for this purpose, the twitch can be placed on the nose and the head elevated with it; or a noose may be put round the upper jaw and then thrown across a beam, so that an attendant can pull the head well up. The bridle should be put on, otherwise the noose may slip out of the mouth. Sometimes a two-pronged fork raises the head by means of a halter, but it is a dangerous practice to use a sharp-pointed fork for such purposes. The great secret in the administration of liquids to the horse is to give them slowly and to keep the head well elevated during the time the animal has the fluid in its mouth. Special appliances are sold for drenching horses, but, no matter whatever appliances be used, abuse must not be resorted to. Some horse-keepers resort to the pernicious practice of pinching and striking the throat, whereas, others, in order to cause the animal to swallow quickly, pour a little fluid down the nostril. If a horse should hold the medicine within its mouth for a long time—a habit which some horses acquire—the best plan is to roll the fingers beneath the tongue, or manipulate that organ in some other way, so as to induce swallowing. A point of importance is that of not allowing the neck of the bottle to pass in between the molar teeth, otherwise it may be bitten off.

A bottle is the best medium for giving the dog liquids, and the neck of this should pass in at a pouch formed by the right cheek, into which the medicine is allowed to trickle. Capsules, pills and powders are in general use for dogs, as also are tabloids, all of which may be placed on the back of the tongue, or concealed rolled up in a piece of meat, butter, etc.

General Management in Disease

Feeding Sick Animals

The feeding of animals when labouring under disease demands a good deal of tact and patience, and there is a wonderful difference between individuals in this respect. One of the worst faults that we are acquainted with is that of allowing food to remain before a sick animal—the presence of which tends to satiate it. Whatever food is given should be in small quantities and often, more especially to horses and dogs, the stomachs of which are small. For sick horses—when procurable—green food is desirable, such as clover, meadow-grass, vetches, lucerne, etc., etc., whilst carrots, swedes or turnips, given whole or grated will often tempt the appetite. A mash composed of linseed, bran and crushed oats, scalded with hot water, if given in small quantities, say, a couple of handfuls at a time, is extremely useful. As artificial nutritive food for the horse, eggs and milk are largely employed, frequently in combination with some stimulant such as whisky, particularly in exhausting diseases as influenza. Eggs and chopped raw meat, Brand's Essence, etc., etc., form excellent nourishment for sick dogs. Horlick's Malted Milk is extremely useful, more especially if the stomach is in an irritated condition, but ordinary milk must be avoided when dogs are troubled with vomiting. Crushed linseed-cake, crushed oats, cabbage, natural grass, cut potatoes and gruel are the usual food substances given to cattle, and one can often bring a cow back to its cud by inserting a cabbage leaf, a piece of potato, etc., between its molar teeth.

Always feed sick animals early in the morning and last thing at night, with additional feeds between, but no food should be allowed to remain before the patient.

Nursing

No matter whatever be the nature of the complaint, good nursing is of paramount importance, and veterinary surgeons are well enough aware of difference in the progress made in the hands of a good, bad or indifferent nurse. Stables and byres should be kept scrupulously clean, and all noxious emanations banished with the aid of disinfectants, pure air, and sunlight. Draughts must be excluded, but stables must not be allowed to be over-heated. An equable, slightly moist atmosphere is the one most desirable. Always have a separate attendant to look after the sick animal, more especially if the disease is of a communicable nature.

Mangers and feeding troughs should be scalded at least once a day, and soiled particles of bedding material instantly removed, and replaced by clean straw. In some diseases affecting the horse, such as lock jaw (tetanus), absolute quietude is an

General Management in Disease

indispensable factor, as the slightest noisy demonstration does, in this complaint, invoke most distressing muscular paroxysms; whilst disturbance causes distress to a horse that is foundered, though it may not be prejudicial. When animals are unconscious (comatose), no effort must be made to force liquid or food down the throat, otherwise the animal may probably be choked. All excrementitious materials should be instantly removed as such may be a source of infection. The natural orifices should be kept clean by constant cleaning with a little antiseptic and water, taking particular care that the sponge is not employed for any other purposes. It must be borne in mind that the nasal discharge in distemper of a horse or dog constitutes an easy means of spreading infection, therefore it should not be allowed to hang about mangers, kennels, clothing, etc. Light horses should have flannel bandages applied to the lower parts of their limbs, as these are of material assistance in maintaining warmth in the lower parts of the extremities.

Use light rugs in summer, heavier ones in winter. Remove these every morning, shake them, and replace.

All short-haired animals are better with their bodies clothed when sick, and a piece of old blanket with four holes cut into it for the limbs will supply the necessary warmth for the smaller ones. Each time the covering is removed, brush the body over; and when horses have any patches of perspiration on them, or irritation, sponge these with a little vinegar and water.

The average temperature of a stable, cowshed, kennel, etc., may be set down at 52° F., but in summer it is difficult to keep it at this, and the clothing must be regulated accordingly. The free use of disinfectants is advisable, and at the close of an infectious disease all fittings should be washed with boiling water and soda; the walls brushed over with a strong solution of carbolic acid, and then limewhitened with fresh lime.

Pheasant coops and ferret hutches should be washed and allowed to dry, and when nearly dry, paraffin oil may be poured over them; lighted, so as to exercise a mild charring influence, thus destroying all parasitic life.

Fomentations and Poultices

The application of either hot or cold water frequently affords a valuable means of reducing various inflammatory processes, both of an internal and external nature. The best method of applying hot water to the belly and chest of horses and cattle is by means of a blanket or woollen rug, steeped in boiling water, then wrung out with a stick applied to each end, and subsequently wrapped round the animal, with a waterproof over all, in order to retain the heat,

General Management in Disease

If prolonged hot fomentations are used the part will be blistered, and it is a good plan on the completion of the fomentation to smear the surface with oil. Hot water rugs require renewal about every ½ hour, and unless persevered in, are not of much use.

For pain in the belly and lung inflammation hot water rugs are a good deal employed. The chief objection being the constant attention requisite in order to maintain the heat.

Mustard paste is largely employed to supplant hot water, being more convenient, and one which many veterinary surgeons consider more efficacious. Mustard paste is formed by mixing 2 parts of mustard with one of linseed meal, with sufficient tepid water to form a paste of the consistency of cream, and is then applied directly to the skin. Its activity can be increased by the addition of white oil or some other stimulating liniment. It may be washed off in a few hours, and reapplied, if necessary, or it can be left on, but it is advisable to apply some stout brown paper over the plastered area, maintaining it in its position with sacking and a binder. The paste may be applied over the whole side of the chest wall, as in lung complaints; on the right side for the liver; on the loins for the kidneys; and over the whole surface of the belly, for abdominal pain. As a substitute for mustard, various blistering liniments are employed, more especially, cantharides.

With long-haired dogs, it is, as a rule, advisable to remove the hair, before the application of the mustard, but linseed and mustard poultices are suitable and should be applied as often as can be tolerated.

For injuries to the feet of horses, it is customary to apply hot bran poultices, linseed poultices, or a combination of the two, and these should be renewed twice daily. Three or four folds of stout sacking, should be sewn together so as to form a sort of jack boot, and a thick layer of poultice put at the bottom and tied on. To supplant poulticing of both horses and cattle, the foot may be allowed to stand in a bucket of hot water, say, for half an hour, to which some antiseptic has been added. For abscesses, bruises, etc., situated externally, the parts should be bathed several times daily with hot water. Sprains about the lower parts of the limbs of horses, say, for the first 12 hours or so can be bathed with cold water, and then a cold water bandage applied over all. After this period hot water may be substituted.

Medicated fomentations are such as have the addition of drugs like arnica, laudanum, lead, etc. and are frequently employed.

THE CAUTERY AND BLISTERING AGENTS

The actual cautery or application of the hot iron is extensively employed by Veterinarians in the

General Management in Disease

treatment of diseases affecting the limbs of the horse, but principally in such diseases as bone-spavin, splint, curb, ringbone, sprained tendons, and other injuries of an allied nature. Both point and line firing are employed. The searing iron is often used after docking, for the purpose of arresting bleeding.

Horses are fired in both the standing and the recumbent attitude, much depending upon the temperament of the animal; the part to be fired; and the severity, or otherwise, of its application.

The indiscriminate use of the firing iron must be condemned, but its universal application is one of its best guarantees of its utility.

Blistering is largely resorted to, and at one time bleeding, blistering and physicing constituted the charlatan's trio of remedies, although such remedial agencies frequently ended, not in the subjugation of the disease, but in the death of the patient.

Before blistering a part, the hair, if long, should be clipped off; the blistering agent then rubbed in for 20 minutes, and the head tied up short for about 48 hours, so as to prevent the animal from biting the part. There is a marked difference in individual horses as to the susceptibility of the action of a blister. In some, blisters will arise within 2 or 3 hours, whilst in others 12 or more hours may elapse.

Cantharides (or spanish fly) is the best blistering

agent; but red iodide of mercury ointment is commonly used, and sometimes a combination of the two. It is not advisable to blister more than two limbs at the same time, and when the lower part of the limb is blistered, some vaseline or lard should be put in the hollow of the heel to prevent blistering the latter.

Firing and blistering are often combined, but the author thinks it is the better plan to delay the application of the blister for a few days after firing.

Setons and rowels both act in a similar way to a blister, and are used for much the same purposes, but also in young stock as a presumed preventative of Black Quarter.

The Slings; Cradle; and Hobbles

These appliances are a good deal in use, and when judiciously employed are of material service.

The slings are employed for horses which require some artificial support, owing to either injury or disease; and very often this appliance is the means of saving an animal's life, but are inapplicable to cattle owing to the ponderous nature of their stomach.

Horses which have a stiff back, and are unable to rise when once they are down, or do so with difficulty, are usually put in slings at night.

Fractures, if amenable to surgical treatment, generally necessitate the use of the slings in the

General Management in Disease

case of horses, and, at times, long periods of repose in slings are necessary.

The best slings are those fitted with the endless chain and pulley, so that the animal can be raised, or lowered by one person.

The cradle is an appliance to fit on the neck of the horse, or, maybe, the dog, and its use to prevent the animal from biting a blistered or inflamed part, which is particularly valuable in the case of the dog, when suffering from skin diseases.

A cradle for the horse can be made with a number of cylindrical pieces of wood, having the same length as the neck and strung together with two stout cords; yet each piece of wood must be separated from its fellows by shorter pieces, forming a sort of necklet at the apex and root of the neck. A stout piece of leather or zinc will do very well for the dog, taking care to have it sufficiently wide to prevent the dog bending its neck in a lateral direction.

The hobbles, shackles, or manacles are used for restraining the animal during the performance of certain painful operations.

A

Abortion

The question that may be asked by the reader is: What is the difference—if such there be—between an abortion and a premature birth?

Conveniently one may reply that an abortion occurs before the sixth month, and the fœtus is either born dead or expires immediately afterwards; whereas a premature birth takes place any time after the sixth month, but before the full period of gestation has arrived, and the fœtus is born alive, and has a chance of surviving, provided that favourable circumstances are present.

There are two forms of abortion, one being called enzoötic (or infective), and the other sporadic, *i.e.* arising without any apparent source of infection. Enzootic abortion is a most troublesome malady amongst cows and ewes, and occasionally in mares. It is due to (according to scientific investigation of the late Professor Frocard) micro-organisms and the infective material or abortion virus is contained within the vaginal discharge, issuing from an infected animal; and when this gains admission into the vaginal mucous membrane of other pregnant animals, it is liable to provoke abortion. The discharge adheres to the hind-quarters; to the tail; etc. and may easily gain admission through the channel named.

Previous to the investigation of Frocard it was thought that abortion arose through sympathy, whereas it is due to infection.

Abortion arises from other causes, such as fright, the action of certain grasses or herbs, external violence, disease of the generative organs, tuberculosis, etc. etc.

General Management in Disease

When abortion appears amongst a herd of cattle or flock of ewes it is absolutely imperative that immediate isolation of the aborters should be enforced, and a separate attendant must be allowed to look after such, as the infection may be conveyed by the clothing of man and various other channels. Most serious losses commonly occur, and every stock keeper knows that when this disease appears, it is uncertain when the trouble will end; and all freshly imported pregnant animals may become infected in a similar manner.

A word of warning may be given, as infectious abortion may easily be introduced into a herd without the owner knowing it.

The advice is to keep all recently purchased in-calf cows by themselves for a period of, say, a month. Abortion arising from accidental causes does not demand these precautionary measures. In dealing with an outbreak of this disease and following upon an immediate isolation of infected animals it is expedient to thoroughly cleanse the hind-quarters, twice or thrice daily, with some antiseptic solution; likewise give vaginal injections of the same, for which it is advisable to consult a veterinary surgeon. The cattle-house or stable should be thoroughly cleaned, disinfected and lime whitened, and as a preventive half an ounce of pure Carbolic Acid may be mixed with bran-mash and given to each cow, along with other food, daily. Half these doses will suffice for a mare.

The Vet. Book

Abdominal Dropsy

Dropsy of the belly is not uncommon in cattle, but perhaps most frequently met with in the dog. It is but symptomatic of disease, usually of a chronic nature. Disease of the liver, or of the kidneys are the most frequent causes of dropsy, but it is also present, in a variable degree, in peritonitis. It is indicative of a grave condition of the constitution. In sheep it is extremely common in the so-called "liver-rot."

Treatment must be left in the hands of the veterinary surgeon, as it comprises surgical and medicinal remedies.

Abdominal Tumours

The question may be asked: "What is a tumour"? It is a difficult matter to define the term, so as to be free from objection, but, roughly speaking, a tumour comprises any unnatural or morbid growth, situated within or without the body.

All morbid growths situate in the cavity of the belly are naturally dangerous, but the issue is influenced by the position of the growth; its size; its nature; and its causation.

In strangles, abscesses occasionally form in connection with the abdominal organs, and sometimes give rise to a fatal inflammation. In all the larger

General Management in Disease

animals operative interference is out of the question, but in the dog, cat, etc. it is a different matter.

Poultry, not uncommonly, have large tumours in the cavity of the belly, and such are generally of a tubercular nature.

Abscess

An abscess consists of a collection of matter, usually of pus, but sometimes of a watery nature, to which the term "serous" is applied.

An abscess results from an infection of the part with pus organisms, and may be the representative of a specific disease as in strangles, blood poisoning etc., or a purely local affection, infection having occurred at this part. When an abscess is situated internally, it is necessarily attended with a considerable amount of danger, and this is why the "irregular" form of Strangles is looked upon as a malady of extreme gravity.

Abscesses vary in their size; situation; and termination.

The so-called "cold abscess" is one that is a long time in arriving at maturity. A "serous" abscess is generally the result of a kick or bruise and a very common form of which occurs on the flap of the dogs' ear; and in cattle about the hind-quarters, side, etc. An abscess of this nature may contain several gallons of a bloody fluid.

Abscesses sometimes attain enormous dimensions, and their favourite situation is in connection with the lymph glands.

Treatment.—Hot fomentations favour the ripening of the abscess; and its maturation is denoted by a soddened feel and pitting on pressure with the finger, due to a gradual thinning of the skin, which, if left to nature, ruptures at this point. But nature increases the area of sloughing, therefore the early use of the lancet is necessary. For serous abscesses, fomentations are no use, but a good blister can be applied, or time allowed for the swelling to arrive at a climax, and then lance it.

Abscess cavities should be washed out with some antiseptic solution and kept open for a few days, but it is preferable to seek professional advice.

Actinomycosis (Timber Tongue)

This disease in cattle often affects the tongue and is known as "timber tongue" or "woody tongue"; but the jaws of cattle are frequently affected, and in America it is commonly spoken of as "lumpy jaw" and in England under the title of "Wens"; being particularly prevalent in the Fen lands of Lincolnshire and Norfolk, but occurs, more or less throughout the British Isles.

The roof of the mouth is sometimes the seat of the disease in cattle, and is denoted by the growth of a deep-red fungoid growth, which gradually extends. But Actinomycosis occasionally involves the skin, more especially about the udder in mares, but, what is still worse, the internal organs may be invaded.

In the horse the spermatic cord is frequently the seat of an allied fungoid disease, producing the so-called "scirrhus-cord," rendering the animal unsound.

This disease is due to the ray fungus or actinomyces, and man is occasionally infected. Professional aid had better be sought.

ACUTE CONGESTION OF THE LUNGS

The horse is a susceptible animal to this malady, and in him it generally arises through severe exertion, brought to bear upon a constitution that has not been prepared for the strain; and this is one reason why it is most frequently encountered in hunters; and in greyhounds, that are run severely without having being brought into condition.

There are other causes, such as noxious emanations arising from an over-heated stable, and more rarely from exposure to cold, as also a change of inflammatory action (Metastasis), such as that from the feet, to the lungs. A phlethoric condition of the body predisposes to this disease, which is not difficult to know, being indicated by rapid and distressed breathing: heaving of the flanks: dilated nostrils: rapid and small pulsations, probably 100 per minute; elevation of internal temperature, and an anxious facial expression. If a hunter, the animal comes to a stand-still and the rider exclaims " bellows to mend!" In a case of this sort the rider must dismount; slacken the girth: turn the animal's head to the wind; and obtain professional advice as speedily as possible.

Acute Inflammation of the Kidneys

One or both kidneys may be the seat of acute inflammatory action: either as an independent affection, or as part of some specific disorder, as in blood-poisoning, etc.

It is a malady attended with danger, and unless properly treated, will end fatally. External violence, and the abuse of such drugs as Spanish Fly, Turpentine, etc., are occasional causes of the trouble. It is denoted by pain in the belly; difficult, or suppressed urinary secretion; pain on pressure of the loins; fever; and all the general signs of ill health.

Hot fomentations may be applied to the loins, pending the arrival of the veterinary surgeon.

Acute Scour in Foals, Lambs, and Calves

This condition is also known as diarrhœa and " white skit " or scour. It is really an acute

A TYPICAL SHORTHORN BULL

General Management in Disease

diarrhœa—the result of infection, and quite different from diarrhœa arising from simple causes.

The source of infection, in most cases, appears to be through the umbilical cord, at or about the time of birth; hence the necessity for due regard to cleanliness, and the use of some mild antiseptic applied to the cord. It is a very exhausting complaint and soon reduces the little creature to a skeleton. But Scour is common in lambs and is, as a rule, due to the presence of either flat or round worms and enzootics are commonly ascribable to this cause. In any case, it is advisable to carefully examine the ejecta, for evidence of segments of tape-worms. Serious losses commonly result through scour, more especially on certain lands, particularly where sewage is distributed.

In chicken-cholera, scour is the predominating sign; and the same remark is applicable to enteric in pheasants.

Yearling colts are troubled with scour, but in these animals it is generally due to either worms, or else through feeding on unsuitable fodder.

If calves and lambs are properly treated, the percentage of deaths should be small.

Treatment.—Begin by giving a dose of Castor Oil, and on the following day give 20 grains of Grey Powder combined with 5 grains of powdered Ipecacuanha and a tea-spoonful of Bicarbonate of Soda, in 3 tablespoonfuls of rice water.

In other cases the treatment will vary in accordance with the causes. Strong tea is a useful "pick-me-up" for sheep and lambs.

AMAUROSIS

This is a disease affecting one or both eyes, and may be either temporary or permanent. The eye is apparently normal, yet the animal is quite blind. It may come on suddenly, through excessive bleeding: through pressure on the optic nerve; such as may result from a tumour, fracture, etc.

ANCHYLOSIS

This term implies stiffening of a joint, and is occasionally observed in the knee of the horse, sometimes as a very severe form of broken knee. It is indicated by a semi-flexed condition of the limb, if at the knee-joint, and is brought about by a gradual obliteration of the joint, either through ossification of the individual bones composing the joint, or through changes in the ligamentous structures in juxtaposition to the joint. Anchylosis of the bones of the back in old horses—chiefly in the region of the loins—is not uncommon, and may prevent the animal from rising; hence the reason why some horses are kept in the slings when not at work. A stiff back is very detrimental to a horse, more especially for saddle purposes.

General Management in Disease

ANEMIA

Under this title a considerable number of ailments are capable of being classified, but in strict pathological language, the term should be limited to a total diminution in the number of red blood cells. Loosely applied, anemia consists of a general bloodless condition of the body; and in some cases is but of a temporary nature, whereas in others it is permanent and incurable, being known as "pernicious" anemia, a disease which has recently been demonstrated to exist in the horse.

Ordinary anemic conditions are benefited by iron compounds, as well as by Cod-Liver Oil and good feeding.

ANGLEBERRIES (*see* Warts)

ANTHRAX

This scourge is one of great antiquity, its existence having been known for several thousands of years, but its true specific nature has only been demonstrated within the last 30 or 40 years.

It is an exceedingly destructive malady, due to the anthrax bacteria, and is liable to affect man; the horse; the ox; the sheep; pig; goat; dog; cat; rabbit; poultry,[1] etc.; in most of which animals it is, as a rule, fatal. An old term for it is, "char-

---

[1] Although it has been said that fowls resist Anthrax, numerous deaths have been recorded of poultry through this disease.

bon," and in man it is known as "malignant pustule" and "wool-sorter's disease"; whilst in cattle the popular name for it is "splenic apoplexy."

There is a closely allied form of the disease which occasionally affects the tongue of the horse and ox, known as "gloss-anthrax," indicated by a swollen condition of that organ, along with blisters upon it, swelling of the head, etc.

Anthrax assumes various forms; sometimes as an acute disease; in other instances, sub-acute; and it is, as a rule, a difficult malady to diagnose during life.

In horses the only evidence of its existence may be severe pain in the belly; elevation of internal temperature, and speedy collapse. As a rule, cattle die very suddenly with it, and the stock-owner may leave his animals apparently well at night, yet find one or more dead on the following morning,—no matter whether they are housed, or at pasture. It is generally the most thrifty members of the herd that succumb, and whenever the proprietor has any sudden losses amongst his stock he should loose no time in reporting the matter to the nearest local authority, which in rural districts may be the Police Officer, as anthrax is a notifiable disease, and its existence, (or suspected existence) demands extreme precautionary measures to be taken in order to guard against, not only the infection of man, but of

General Management in Disease

other animals. Never skin a sheep or ox that dies suddenly unless it is perfectly clear what the cause of the animal's death has been, as many deaths in human beings have occurred through such foolish procedure.

An anthrax carcase; its hide; or any portion thereof; may easily inoculate a man, if he has the most trivial scratch upon his hand, and death frequently occurs from such cause. The death-rate in man may be set down at 40 per cent.

Dogs must not be allowed to feed off such a carcase, as they may infect other animals, although recover from the disease themselves. Anthrax in swine is often denoted by a swollen condition of the throat, though the latter is not necessarily present.

In the cadaver blood often issues from the natural orifices, and this along with the sudden death; drum-like condition of the belly; and rapid decomposition of the carcase; plus *negative* evidence of death from other causes, is the best practical proof of death for anthrax. Veterinary Surgeons usually cut off a portion of the ear and mount films of the blood for microscopic examination to find the anthrax bacteria, and this opinion has to be confirmed by the Board of Agriculture. The legislative measure for controlling the proprietor's conduct in anthrax are very strict, and all bodies have to be cremated under the direction of the Veterinary Inspector, and at the expense of the Local Authority.

Aphtha

This comprises a vasicular eruption inside the mouth, more especially upon the tongue of horses and cattle, but there is a specific aphtha, known as Foot and Mouth Disease, which is, fortunately, non-existent in Great Britain and Ireland.

Apoplexy of the Lungs (*see* Congestion of Lungs)

Apoplexy Parturient (*see* Parturient Apoplexy)

Apoplexy of the Brain

An apoplectic stroke occasionally occurs in domestic animals and is denoted by the suddenness of attack. It is due to a rupture of a minute blood vessel in connection with the brain. Loss of consciousness, loss of motor power, and the involuntary passage of urine, etc., are usually present.

External injuries, such as, a fall upon the skull, a blow, etc., may produce a similar state of affairs.

Treatment must be left to the Veterinary Surgeon, though it is generally fatal.

Arteries, Injuries to (*see* Wounds)

Arsenical Poisoning

When given with criminal intent, Arsenic constitutes a corrosive poison, and many deaths in horses have been recorded, through horse-keepers giving this chemical to horses to improve the condition of coat and wind, though usually unknown to their masters.

The average medicinal dose of Arsenious Acid for the horse is 4 grains, but horse keepers have given as much as would lie upon a sixpence, which has produced a condition of the system, known as "tolerance," though acute arsenical poisoning is liable to occur at any time.

The average dose for the dog is the $\frac{1}{30}$ of a grain, but it is commonly given to this animal in the form of Fowler's Solution of Arsenic.

In the horse, the leading symptoms are; pain in the belly; purgation and collapse; whilst in the dog, vomiting is super-added to these. The correct antidote is freshly prepared Hydrated Peroxide of Iron, with a reasonable amount of stimulants.

It must be mentioned that many sheep-dips and weed-killers are largely composed of arsenical compounds, and many accidental deaths in poultry, etc., are attributable to the careless use of such substances.

Ascarides (*see* Worms)

Asthma

This affection is most frequently met with in the dog. It seems to be due to a spasmodic contraction of the muscular fibres of the bronchial tubes, and is of an intermittent nature.

In the dog it is denoted by suddenness of seizure, the animal being attacked with a rapid series of inspiratory movements, as though in fear of impending suffocation. Aged dogs that are very fat and indolent are the most frequent sufferers, and is often associated with a torpid condition of the bowels. It is practically incurable, in all animals, and much the same as in man.

B

BELLADONNA

Atropa Belladonna or the Deadly Night-shade is a poisonous perennial, sending up annual shoots, bearing thin ovate leaves, flowering in the Autumn. The flowers are a dusky brown; bell-shaped; and the fruit consists of green berries whilst unripe, which subsequently turn black. Both the leaves and fruit are exceedingly poisonous, containing an active principle known as Atropine. Medicinal extracts are prepared from both leaves and root.

Belladonna causes widening of sphincter muscles, hence the pupil becomes dilated, and other sphincters relaxed.

BITES AND STINGS

Both these accidents are liable to occur, more especially in the horse and dog. When dogs are

General Management in Disease

bitten during fighting, etc., their wounds should be examined at once, and dressed with an antiseptic, as many of such are, apparently, only trifling externally, though, in reality, there may be extensive tearing of the muscles beneath.

Bee stings sometimes prove fatal to horses. The best application is a solution of Ammonia. Powder Blue for stings also useful.

BLADDER, INFLAMMATION OF

Inflammation of the bladder is a serious disease, and is capable of arising as an extension of inflammation from adjacent parts; from external injuries; from the use of irritating drugs; from stone within it. It is indicated by pain in the belly; painful urination; switching of the tail, fever, and general signs of illness.

Hot fomentations may be applied to the extreme back part of the belly, but the sooner professional aid is obtained the better.

BLADDER, STONE WITHIN

Although all animals are liable to calculi within the bladder, the dog is probably the most frequent sufferer, and this may be due to a large amount of phosphates contained in the urine.

There may be a single calculus or a number of same, and such vary in their shape, size, etc., Sometimes a single large calculus will occupy the whole cavity of the bladder, whereas in other cases it is more of a gravelly nature. Stone is indicated by difficult or suppressed urination; pain, and loss of energy. The treatment is purely surgical.

Bleeding

In certain inflammatory disorders, the abstraction of blood is sometimes resorted to, principally in horses and cattle, for the purpose of relieving congestion. About $\frac{1}{2}$ a gallon of blood is the usual quantity to abstract, and the jugular vein at its upper third is the usual seat of operation.

The Fleam is the instrument used, and the vein is pinned and tied after the blood has been removed. In acute congestion of the Lungs, in a healthy animal, full bleeding is unquestionably beneficial. (*See also* Hæmorrhage.)

Bloody Flux (*see* Dysentery)

Blood Poisoning

This is rather an ambiguous term, and includes many morbid conditions; such as anthrax, black-quarter, mortification, etc., but it is better to limit the meaning of the term to a pyæmic infection, following upon the introduction of septic material from without, and denoted by the formation of multiple abscesses, in various parts of the body, internally and externally.

General Management in Disease

It is necessarily a disease attended with a large amount of danger, demanding professional skill for its treatment. (*See* Mortification.)

BLOOD SPAVIN (*see* Bone Spavin)

BOG SPAVIN

This is a loose term, but most horsemen are familiar with it, as a puffy condition of the hock joint, the degree of distension being variable. It does not necessarily constitute unsoundness, and some horses have a puffy condition of the hock on the morning following active work.

It is apparently due to a hyper-secretion of synovia, or joint oil, probably through some weakness of the capsular ligament of the joint. Only when it becomes excessive need it be looked upon unfavourably. Blistering will do good, but firing is better, though not always curative, at any rate, permanently.

BONE SPAVIN

A bone spavin comprises a variable-sized deposit of bone, situated upon the inner and lower aspect of the hock, or hocks, in accordance whether one, or both hocks, are affected.

The Spavin represents nature's method of repair and in some cases a spavined hock is stronger than before; whereas, in other instances, more especially in old horses, the animal becomes permanently lame. By many spavin is regarded as a hereditary disease, and it is well known that hocks that are narrow or tied in below, are more liable to develop bone spavin than those without such conformation. The size of the spavin is no criterion as to the degree of lameness it may produce, because some very small spavins give rise to most intractable forms of lameness, whereas very large ones are often unoffensive.

All forms of bone-spavin, legally, constitute unsoundness and Veterinary Surgeons must reject such horses, but if a horse has good strong hocks, is free from lameness, and turned five years old, required for slow work only, such an animal may be passed as "practically" sound, but, of course, the vendor ought to make some reduction in the price.

A hock may be spavined and yet afford no appreciable evidence of such, and litigation has sometimes arisen under these circumstances, but the onus of responsibility does not, in a case of this nature, rest with the examiner of the animal. This condition is known as "occult" spavin. A blood spavin, on the other hand, is merely a distended condition of a vein as it passes over the front of the hock, but is not regarded as an unsoundness. The best method of detecting a bone-spavin—also known as a "Jack"—is to view the hock obliquely from the front and com-

General Management in Disease

pare it with its fellow, when the slightest enlargement will be detected.

Prolonged rest and firing, afford the principal means of dealing with spavin lameness.

THE HORSE BOT-FLY

This fly is commonly about during hay-time, and the female deposits her eggs upon the hairs,

Eggs of Bot Fly on Horse's Hair (Magnified)   Fundament or Red Bot   Stomach Bot   Female Bot Fly

BOTS

especially about the knees, shoulders, and arms of the horse. The eggs closely resemble "nits," and adhere to the hairs through the medium of a sticky substance. In due course maggots are hatched, and these cause the horse some irritation, hence it licks the seat of attack, and the maggots are taken into the stomach and fix themselves on to the gullet end of the lining of the stomach, assuming a barrel shape. Unless very numerous, they don't do any harm. The following spring

53

they are passed out with the ejecta, remain hidden in the ground for a few weeks, and then develop into the full-blown fly. The Ox Bot-Fly deposits its eggs beneath the skin as "Warbles."

When these flies are about it is better to smear the favourite egg-laying places with some strong-smelling smear, such as Tar Ointment, etc.

Bowels, Inflammation of

Acute inflammation of the bowels is a common complaint, especially in horses, and arises from a variety of causes. In some instances, it is produced by the organisms of anthrax; in others by worms; irritant poisons; extension of inflammatory action; external injuries; concretions within the bowel, and other agencies.

Dogs are also frequent sufferers, and the principal cause arises from the presence of round worms, and a considerable percentage of puppies die from inflammation of the bowels thus induced. A twisted bowel and an intussuscepted (telescoped) bowel, are common causes of inflammation, and it is quite possible that both these conditions may arise from worm irritation, or obstruction by such.

In splenic apoplexy of cattle (anthrax), and braxy of sheep, the bowels are often acutely inflamed.

Peritonitis is frequently associated with enteritis

General Management in Disease

(inflammation of the bowels). The leading symptoms of this disease are: acute pain in the belly, of a continuous character; a quick, small and hard pulse; and in dogs, vomiting sometimes. Horses roll; sit upon their haunches; and when, the pain is excessively severe—as in strangulation of the large gut—the patient may attempt to climb the wall of the box, and scream with pain. The stormy character of the disease sometimes leads to death within an hour or two, whereas, in other cases, the animal may continue in pain for days, and then succumb.

An amateur may easily confuse this with simple functional colic, or the converse; therefore it shows how very necessary it is to seek professional advice early. In any case inflammation of the bowels in the horse, etc., is always fatal.

Braxy

This term is commonly applied to disease affecting sheep and derives its name from "Broc" or "Brac," terms used by hill shepherds as indicating disease of any kind, though, in reality, it is a very meaningless term. All sorts of pathological conditions, such as diarrhœa; anthrax; dysentery; constipation; etc. etc. may be classified as synonymous with braxy.

Shepherds should exercise particular care when

handling an animal affected with braxy, because it may have anthrax, and infection occur if the shepherd has any slight abrasion on his hands.

Never skin a braxied sheep. Neither ought the flesh to be eaten, as such is attended with considerable risk to human life.

Many people eat braxied flesh, and it is quite common to find a piece of braxied mutton dried and hanging up in the homesteads of Scottish crofters. Wet, dry, and dumb forms of braxy have been described, but the clinical significance attachable thereto, is of no particular importance.

Broken Wind

This pathological condition is confined to the horse, and is of common occurrence. It is denoted by a characteristic cough which, once heard, is easily recognised a second time. It is a peculiar hollow cough. In addition to the cough, the breathing furnishes evidence of broken wind. The act of inspiration is performed normally, but the expiratory efforts abnormally. The last-named is *double*, constituting the so-called "double lift." Expiratory effort is divided into two portions: the first part of the act being to expel the air as normally, but, in the second portion of it, the remainder of the air in the chest is apparently *squeezed out of it* in a gradual manner. Commercially speaking a broken-winded horse has

General Management in Disease

no value, yet it may continue to perform its work fairly well. The cough may be disguised by an unprincipled vendor through the administration of such substances as shot and grease; but this is only temporary, and, of course, the abnormal breathing cannot be disguised. In some cases of broken wind, the air-vesicles of the lungs have been found, after death, ruptured; and the walls of the stomach dilated, though this is not constant.

BROKEN KNEES (*see* Wounds)

BRONCHITIS

Inflammation of the bronchial tubes is frequent amongst all classes of animals, and sometimes exists simply as Bronchitis, but much more frequently in combination with other diseases of the lung, such as, tuberculosis; glanders; catarrhal pneumonia, etc. The large or the small tubes may be involved, and as long as the inflammation remains confined to the larger bronchial tubes, there is not much danger; but when the capillary tubes are implicated there is the risk of catarrhal pneumonia developing. Atmospherical; chemical; mechanical; and specific cause, are the chief agents operative in the production of bronchitis. The bronchitic râle is pathognomonic of the malady, and is due to the passage of air through the liquid in the tubes.

Both in distemper in the dog, and influenza in

the horse, bronchitis—though of a variable degree—is often present. Mechanical bronchitis arises through the inhalation of irritating vapour, also through the presence of thread-worms in the air-tubes, so common in calves, sheep, poultry, and pheasants, etc., constituting Hoose and Gapes.

Management.—The most important factor is an equable moist atmosphere. The inhalation of medicated steam affords a valuable means of bringing the medicament into direct contact with the air-tubes. A little Oil of Eucalyptus, Camphor, and Turpentine are the best drugs for the purpose.

For the dog, hot linseed poultices can be applied to the chest; and in cattle and horses, mustard-paste; but the principles of treatment must be left to the superior judgment of the veterinary attendant.

Bruises

A bruise represents the effects of some form of external violence, applied directly or indirectly, producing an extravasation of blood within the tissues, with or without rupture of muscular fibres, and in some cases it is accompanied by a fracture (*q.v.*) Evaporating lotions, such as ½ pt. of Methylated Spirit, combined with 1 oz. of Laudanum, and 4 oz of Opodeldoc, are most useful for such purposes. Bruises and contusions are practically of the same nature, and require

General Management in Disease

similar treatment. The application of hot water is most useful for both, after the swelling has come on, but the evaporating lotion is the correct application, *immediately after* the infliction of the injury.

Burns

A burn is a superficial and, in some cases, deep injury to the skin and subjacent structures. Horses are sometimes extensively burned through fire, and sometimes through lime. Hot water is an occasional cause in the dog and cat. When the burn is extensive it is a good plan to paint it with Tincture of Iodine, and then coat it over with lime-water, and whitening to exclude the air.

Another useful application is 1 part of Oil of Eucalyptus, to 12 parts of Olive Oil. Sometimes it is necessary to give a little sedative medicine internally, such as a few doses of Bromide of Potash, say ½ oz. for a horse, and 20 grains for a dog, there times per day.

Bursal Enlargements (Windgall, etc.)

Swellings of the class occur in both horses and cattle, but such are exceedingly common in the horse. Synonymous terms are " windgall," " bog spavin." A bursal enlargement may occur wherever there is a synovial bursa or tendinous sheath, and such swellings are common about the fetlocks, hocks, knees, etc., varying in their size, and form.

In some cases, they are developed through hard wear, and are sometimes indicative of the horse having performed a lot of work either before it has reached maturity, or later on in life.

A frequent situation to find a bursal enlargement in cattle is at the knee, and this consists of a distended condition of the sheath of the extensor metacarpai magnus tendon. It arises through intermittent pressure.

Bursal enlargements can be treated in a simple manner by coating them over with common gas-tar, and repeating this every two or three weeks.

Blistering and firing, also puncturing, are employed by veterinarians for their reduction.

C

Canker of the Foot

This is a most troublesome complaint, and may affect one or more of the feet. It is denoted by a fungoid growth of horn about the frog and sole, and in advanced cases the wall of the hoof becomes implicated. A most offensive odour is emitted. There is no difficulty in recognising the disease.

In some cases it causes lameness, and it is looked upon as a criminal offence to work a horse with canker of the foot, which is practically an incurable disease, or, at any rate, one that demands

A YOUNG LONGHORN BULL

General Management in Disease

more than ordinary patience and skill for its cure. It can be kept in check by pressure and the use of antiseptics combined with astringents.

Use a powder composed of ½ oz. each of Copperas and Blue-stone, along with the same quantity of Alum and Boracic Powder, daily.

CANKER OF THE EAR

Both dogs and cats are troubled with this disease, which affects the middle ear, being an inflammation of its lining membrane, accompanied by a variable degree of suppuration; but there is also a parasitic form of canker, which is indicated by a sooty-like deposit in the ear.

In the cat, convulsions sometimes accompany it, and a serous abscess of the cartilage of the ear occasionally exists, as an addition.

When a dog has canker of the ear it turns its head to one side, or alternately to the right and left when both ears are affected, and the discharge may be tinged with blood; of an offensive nature; causing the animal a considerable degree of discomforture.

In some cases, the cause is constitutional, and patches of eczema occasionally co-exist. The ear should be cleaned with Methylated Spirits of Wine and water, and then dressed with some antiseptic, combined with a mild astringent.

Dust the inside of the ear with a powder composed of ½ oz. Boracic Acid, 1 drachm of

Alum, 20 grains of Calomel, and 20 grains of Iodoform.

To prevent shaking of the ear, apply a many-tailed bandage.

"*External*" *canker* of the ear is simply a wound on the flap of the ear, which has little inclination to heal, and is difficult to cure. The thickened edges of the wound must be removed with the fingers, and then the sore smeared with Venice Turpentine.

Capped Elbow

The old terms "capulet" and "shoe-boil" are still employed by some as indicative of this malady, which consists of a bruise at the point of the elbow, generally caused by the inner heel of the shoe, though sometimes by the outer, and sometimes from other causes. It corresponds to capped hock, and the continued irritation leads to the production of a variable sized fibroid tumour. The skin may be broken, and slight suppuration very often occurs. The cause must be removed, and the animal compelled to wear a leather or rubber ring round the fetlock, whilst in the stable. The rest of the treatment is of a surgical nature.

Capped Hock (*see* Hocks, Capped)

Cartilages, Ossified (*see* Side Bone)

General Management in Disease

CATARACT

This is a disease affecting the crystalline lense, its capsule, or both; and not at all uncommon in horses and dogs, more especially aged animals. A blow over the eye, and other causes occasion it. It is practically incurable.

CATARRH

A catarrhal affection is one denoted by a variable degree of congestion of the mucous membranes, more especially those lining the nasal chamber; and eyes; but other organs may be affected. As a simple affection, catarrh is common in all animals, usually running a short course, followed by complete restoration to health; but there is a malignant form of catarrh affecting cattle, and this is a malady of a more serious nature.

Catarrhal symptoms constitute one of the classical features of distemper and influenza, being almost constantly present in these maladies.

Whatever irritates the nasal mucous membrane may lead to a catarrhal congestion of it, and chronic forms of catarrh are generally present in such diseases as glanders; caries of the molar teeth; diseases of the air-sinuses, etc. etc.

Simple catarrh, or coryza (cold in the head) is denoted by a redness and dryness of the mucous membrane, followed by a hyper-secretion from the nose. Redness of the eyes; general lassitude; and other minor signs of ill-health are present.

All that is necessary is that of keeping the animal warm, and to give a mild purge.

Chest Founder

This is synonymous with kennel lameness, and rheumatism (which see).

Chapped Heels

Cracked heels are frequent in the horse, especially following a frost, the moisture from the thaw favouring this. This condition corresponds to chapped hands, and fissuring is favoured by the movements in the hollow of the heels.

Cracked heels are denoted by an inflamed condition of the skin, which subsequently becomes broken, and, if severe, may lead to lameness.

When a draught, such as beneath the bottom of a door, is allowed to play upon the heated skin of the heel, it leads to congestion of it.

The application of astringents is not advisable, but some soothing agent, such as a liniment composed of 3 oz. of Glycerine and 2 drachms of Goulard's Water, will do good, if applied daily, with tow and a bandage.

General Management in Disease

Chorea (Twitch, Jumps, St Vitus' Dance)

The dog is the most frequent sufferer from this complaint, which in 99 cases out of every 100 exists as a sequel to distemper.

It is denoted by an involuntary twitching of the muscles, and may be confined to some particular region, such as the head, limbs, etc., or distributed over the body. It is practically incurable.

Shivering in the horse is an allied condition, and also incurable. The causes of chorea are variable and the pathology of an obscure nature.

Chronic Cough

The term chronic cough is applied to such coughing efforts as are of a permanent nature in the horse, and is symptomatic of disease, either in the respiratory apparatus, stomach, etc. Thus, for instance, the cough is chronic in broken wind, glanders, etc. It constitutes unsoundness.

Coffin Bone (Fractured)

This bone is lodged within the hoof, and in exceptional instances it gets broken through external violence. In some cases the fracture has been preceded by caries (disease) of the bone.

Colic (*see* Gripes)

CONCRETIONS IN THE INTESTINES

Concretions in the intestines of the horse are by no means uncommon.

They vary in their size, shape, and number, but the most dangerous are those about the size of a cricket-ball, as these are apt to wander and completely block up some narrow portion of the gut, more especially the floating colon and the rectum. Large concretions may attain the size of a cannon-ball, and enormous numbers have been removed from horses, the smaller ones being frequently passed per anus. A concretion has usually a foreign body for a nucleus, and growth is by accretion. They are frequent causes of colic and enteritis.

CONTRACTED FEET

The contraction of the foot or feet is not a diseased condition of itself, but symptomatic of such, and leads to undesirable consequences. Directly the full functions of the foot are removed the hoof begins to shrink (or contract), more especially towards the heels, and contracted feet are regarded by veterinary surgeons as constituting unsoundness.

Lameness soon leads to contraction, and so does the removal of frog pressure; hence the reason why the smith should never pare the frog.

General Management in Disease

Corns

A corn consists of a bruise to the sensitive sole, and shows itself in the form of a reddish discoloration of the horny sole beneath the bruise, and usually appears upon the inner quarter of the fore-foot, very rarely on the hind; but there is practically no difference between a bruise in this, and other parts of the sole. When a corn has been in existence for a few days it turns a reddish brown, and sometimes a greenish yellow, more especially the last-named, if suppuration has begun (suppurating corn).

A corn very often causes severe lameness, and is looked upon as a cause of unsoundness.

The part should be pared, and the shoeing attended to. If suppuration has occurred it must be allowed to have free exit, otherwise it will break out at the coronet, and end in quittor.

Poultice the foot with hot linseed and bran, and keep thoroughly clean. Rest for a week or so.

Crib-Biting

This is an objectionable habit, and frequently accompanied by wind-sucking. If so, the objection is increased. Once acquired, it is a difficult matter to wean a horse off it, but plenty of work is, to some extent, a preventative, or the animal may be fed off the ground, or in a swinging manger, etc.

Curb

Both light and heavy horses are subject to curb, which is a variable sized enlargement, about 3 inches below the point of the hock, lying in the same straight line; and frequently produced by a sprain of the ligament at the back of the hock. One or both hocks may be curby, and the curbs unequal in size. It is not often that curb causes lameness, and when it does so it is chiefly during its formative stage. It is legally an unsoundness, but certainly not much of a detriment, especially in a horse required for slow work. Is easily detected by viewing the limb in profile, when the slightest undulation just below the point of the hock, will be seen if curb is present.

Cutting

The term cutting is applied when a horse strikes the hind fetlock of the opposite limb, usually with the shoe, producing an injury to the skin. Striking or interfering are synonymous terms, but "speedy cutting" is quite a different injury (*see* Speedy Cutting).

Defective conformation often leads to cutting and is sometimes a very difficult matter to remedy.

Various devices have been employed to stop it, and the most common one is the use of a feather-edged shoe or a three-quarter shoe; but these are often quite useless for such purposes.

General Management in Disease

Sometimes the outer heel requires lowering. A boot or pad is often fixed around the fetlock to guard against this injury.

D

Depraved Appetite

This is usually symptomatic of digestive disorder, and animals affected in this way are not as a rule thrifty. One of the commonest causes in the dog is the presence of worms in the intestines.

Some animals will eat all sorts of foreign substances, and these, especially in cattle, are the occasional cause of death. Treatment accordingly.

Diabetes

In this disorder there is an excessive discharge of urine, usually of pale colour, accompanied with a voracious appetite, and abnormal thirst. There is a simple form of diabetes, very common in horses, usually arising through feeding on damaged fodder. It is known as Diabetes insipidus, in contra-distinction to Saccharine Diabetes, which is an uncommon disease in the horse.

Dogs are occasionally troubled with the latter form of diabetes, and in them it is incurable, whilst ordinary diabetes is very often present in Tuberculosis of the horse.

When due to musty hay, or overheated oats, the withdrawal of the food, and suitable treatment soon lead to recovery, in the simpler form of diabetes. Iodine is almost a specific for this, but a veterinary surgeon should be consulted at once.

Diarrhœa

Liquid evacuations are symptomatic of many disorders, and it is only by removing the source of irritation that a cure may be hoped for. Exposure to cold, presence of worms, unsuitable food, too much grass, sudden changes of diet, excessive doses of purgative medicine, infection and hyper-acidity of the stomach, rank amongst the principal causes.

The frequent passage of liquid evacuations must be looked upon as a salutary process, being Nature's method of ridding the economy of the offending material. In lambs it is often due to worms (*see* Scour). The same remark applies to colts (*see* also Scour in Calves and Foals).

Simple diarrhœa can often be checked with chlorodyne given in 20 drop doses for dogs, and $\frac{1}{2}$ oz. doses for horses every four hours.

The food must be changed, and should be easy of digestion; milk and arrowroot being useful for the smaller animals.

General Management in Disease

Dislocations

Either an organ, such as the eye, or a bone entering into the formation of a joint may be displaced from its normal position. If so, it is called a dislocation. In the horse the stifle-joint is not uncommonly the seat of such injury; the patella, or knee-cap, being displaced to either the inner or the outer side, causing the animal to drag the limb. The eye-ball of the dog is occasionally dislocated.

Distemper (Influenza in Horse)

Distemper of the dog, and of the horse (influenza) is exceedingly common, and all horsemen and kennelmen are familiar with this scourge, which has been in existence for centuries, causing untold losses.

It is a specific, eruptive, febrile disease in the dog, but the eruption does not occur in the horse.

The disease is highly infectious and transmitted through multifarious channels, such as feeding utensils, clothing, bedding, water-troughs, etc. Ferrets, weasels, stoats, foxes, etc., all suffer from it, and may transmit it to the dog.

Spring and autumn are the seasons when it is most prevalent, and young dogs are the most frequent sufferers; one attack conferring a degree, though not absolute, immunity.

Distemper in the dog and influenza in the horse,

though allied, present many clinical differences, which it is not herein necessary to discuss. When the disease appears in an adult dog, the animal withstands the attack better.

The earliest indications of distemper are afforded by the clinical thermometer, which shows a rise of several degrees, in fact this is the best method for the early detection of the malady.

The membranes lining the eye-lids are heightened in colour, the nose hot and dry, the mouth dry; and the animal has shivering fits; seeking the warmest corner of its kennel; is dull, has little inclination for food, and in due course becomes very thirsty. This is soon followed by a watery discharge from the nose and eyes, and as the disease advances the discharge becomes of a creamy nature.

As a rule there is a troublesome cough; and the dog makes repeated attempts to dislodge mucus from the throat. It is a peculiar but characteristic husky cough. In addition to the foregoing there may be bronchitis; pleurisy; pneumonia; or liver disorder; with or without diarrhœa; dysentery; etc. etc.

Sometimes fits are present in the distemper of the dog, and not uncommonly paralysis supervenes; if so, the chances of recovery are materially diminished.

Very much the same features are present in the influenza of the horse, and in both animals a

General Management in Disease

striking characteristic is marked prostration, with rapid loss of flesh.

Rheumatic complications are not uncommon in the horse, and when the liver is implicated it is spoken of as the *bilious* form, whilst a swollen condition of the mucous membranes of the eyelids confers the title of " pink-eye."

Both diseases usually run their course within two or three weeks, but complications prolong the malady.

Management.—Affected animals must be kept warm and isolated; body should be clothed, and the limbs of light horses bandaged.

To the dog it is advisable to give an emetic such as from 2 to 6 drachms of Ipecacuanha Wine. This will usually relieve the cough.

The discharge from the nose, in both horses and dogs, must be encouraged, and this can be done by steaming the nostrils with medicated steam, night and morning.

Stimulants are necessary, and there is nothing better than frequently repeated small doses of whisky combined with eggs. Linseed gruel is particularly suitable for the horse; and if the cough is a troublesome feature of the disease, in this animal, it is advisable to blister the throat.

If dog is troubled with fits, give from 10 to 30 grains Bromide of Ammonia, in a little water, three times per day; whilst if it is dysentery, give 10 grains of Grey Powder once a day.

The Vet. Book

Good nursing and an absolute regard for strict hygienic measures will be found indispensable.

As nourishment for dogs, Brand's essence, beaten up eggs, and a very small amount of raw meat given four or five times a day will do good. Wincarnis is of service as a tonic and restorative; so is strong coffee.

The chief danger is in connection with the complications, more especially pleurisy, hence the necessity for seeking professional advice.

DYSENTERY

In this disease the liquid evacuations are accompanied with a discharge of blood, and it is known to cattlemen and shepherds under the title of bloody flux.

In some cases it is a specific disease, whereas in others it arises from irritants.

The lower end of the rectum is chiefly the seat of the disease, therefore dysentery can sometimes be checked by injections into the lower end of the bowels.

A tablespoonful of boiled starch, combined with a teaspoonful of Hazeline and $\frac{1}{2}$ drachm of Laudanum is useful in the case of the dog. Powdered Ipecacuanha is an excellent remedy, but quite recently a serum has been introduced for the treatment of this disease in man, and it is possible that it will become applicable to animals.

General Management in Disease

E

Eczema

This is a very common complaint amongst dogs, though occasionally occurring in other animals—more especially the horse.

It consists of a superficial inflammation of the skin, produced by a variety of causes, but in the majority of instances it is due to congestion of the liver; to irritation of the digestive organs, and kidney derangements; which, in turn, disturb the nervous mechanism supplying the skin with normal activity. External irritants sometimes produce eczematous patches, and the dog aggravates the complaint by scratching and licking the part. Most cases of eczema are constitutional in their origin and require internal treatment, therefore such organs as the liver and kidneys should be got into proper working order. There is an acute and chronic form of the disease, and the latter frequently appears in the horse at the inside of the knee; in front of the hock, being known as Mallenders and Sallenders respectively, which is a troublesome disease to cure. It occurs on the points of the hock and buttocks in the dog.

Treatment for acute eczema.—If in patches apply Boracic Ointment, but if chronic rub with Tar Ointment daily, and give internally a dose of a laxative medicine. For dogs, give 3 to 10 drops of Arsenic in food once or twice a day for three weeks, then give another dose of purgative medicine.

ENTERITIS (*see* Abdominal pain)

EPILEPSY

Epileptic fits and convulsions occur very frequently in the dog and in an allied form in horses and cattle occasionally; and it is quite possible that megrims in the horse is sometimes of this nature.

Epileptic fits frequently come on during distemper, and their onset is unquestionably favoured by some form of irritation within the alimentary canal, frequently by worms. Teething convulsions occur in puppies, but dogs of an irritable temperament are predisposed to become troubled with epilepsy.

External injuries, such as some form of pressure upon the brain, may lead to fits. Nervous phenomena sometimes appear through sun-stroke (pseudo-epilepsy). The symptoms are suddenness of attack; twitching of the muscles of face and mouth; champing of the jaws, causing foaming at the mouth, temporary loss of consciousness, and falling to the ground. In some cases the animal rushes madly about, and the ignorant are apt to confuse it with rabies. The animal, in some cases, remains unconscious for several days, and then may recover.

General Management in Disease

Treatment.—The bowels must be relieved at once with an enema and a dose of laxative medicine. Sedatives, such as Bromide of Ammonium, from 10 to 30 grains in a little water, should be given twice or thrice daily. Animal must be kept quiet, and not allowed to injure itself.

ERYTHEMA (SORE SHOULDERS, SADDLE GALLS, etc.)

This is a superficial congestion of the skin, and the preliminary to nearly all skin diseases It is denoted by redness and excoriation.

Saddle and collar galls are of this nature, and frequently give rise to a good deal of inconvenience, and suffering to the animal.

It is a penal offence to work an animal with this injury, unless the source of irritation has been removed, *i.e.* the pressure.

When a horse gets into poor condition, the angularities about the shoulders, back, etc., predispose the skin to become galled, but the fault is generally due to badly fitting harness; and this should always be looked to. The collar may be hollowed out over the injury, or padded with wool. Some horses will chafe their skin very easily, and it appears to be constitutional. Bad conformation of the shoulders tends to produce it, but sudden cooling of the skin, through removal of the collar, saddle, etc., immediately the animal comes in from work, leads to conjestion, and subsequent excoriation. The best preventative is to leave these on, for about an hour.

When the skin has been bruised, apply an evaporating lotion (*see* Bruises). Methylated Spirit will harden the skin.

Eye (*see* Inflammation of)

Eyelids, Torn (*see* Wounds)

F

Falling of the Womb (*see* Prolapsus Uteri)

False Quarter

This is an indentation, or furrow in the wall of of the hoof, usually observed in the fore foot of the horse. It is due to a defective secretion of the horn: predisposes to sand-crack, and constitutes unsoundness.

Farcy (*see* Glanders)

Fetlock Joint (Sprain of)

The fetlock joint of a horse is occasionally the seat of a sprain. If so there is lameness, increased heat and swelling, which may persist for some days.

When the joint is manipulated, it causes the animal pain. Rest, and the application of cooling lotion, followed by hot water, will be of service.

SOUTH DOWN COW

General Management in Disease

Fistula (*see* Withers)

Flatulent Colic (*see* also Gripes)

The term flatulent colic is applied when an attack of colic is accompanied by an accumulation of gas, causing a drum-like sound to be emitted, when the area between the last ribs, and angle of the haunch, is struck. Gaseous accumulation is due to the fermentation of food, and it sometimes accumulates so rapidly that the animal may succumb within half an hour. Hence the necessity for veterinary aid, with all speed. Meanwhile the flanks should be vigorously shampooed; and the animal compelled to move briskly about; whilst cold water may be applied to the loins and flank.

Two oz. of Turpentine and 1 pt. Linseed Oil may be given in the meantime.

Flexor Tendon (Sprain of)

The flexors are situated at the back of the limbs, and very often are sprained, and such may lead to permanent thickening, and contraction of the limb, causing the animal to go on its toe.

Old standing sprains are incurable, and for recent ones it is better to have veterinary advice. The ligaments at the back of the knee are often sprained, more especially the inferior-check ligament.

Fluke Disease (*see* Liver rot)

Foot Punctured

The horse commonly suffers from this injury, which may be due to a picked up nail, or to one which has been falsely driven by the shoeing-smith. In the latter case, in order to prove damage, the proprietor must show proof of negligence, but when horses are troublesome to shoe, the fault may not be attributable to the smith.

Lock-jaw frequently follows injury to the feet; therefore it is advisable to have professional aid.

Too much attention cannot be paid to injuries of this nature, and one of the commonest sequels to such is quittor. The shoe should be removed, the seat of the injury well-pared out, and a hot linseed and bran poultice applied night and morning, and the foot bathed with some antiseptic solution.

Foot-rot and Foul

Foot-rot is a disease affecting the feet of sheep; and foul, an allied condition, frequently observed in the feet of cattle.

It is exceedingly common amongst sheep pastured on low-lying ground, more especially in wet weather, and once it makes its appearance, it is a constant source of trouble.

There is a contagious form of it, which causes

General Management in Disease

most serious inconvenience, and loss to the flockmaster.

In the early stages of disease the skin—a little above the claws is white and moist, covered with pimples, whilst later on the inflammation extends to the inner side of the claw, and the hoof becomes completely undermined with matter, forming a condition corresponding to "whitlow," and in due course the claw may be cast off. When foot-rot is neglected, complete disorganisation of the foot occurs: the animal becomes very lame, loses flesh rapidly, and is found grazing upon one or both knees.

Foul begins in the inter digital space, and is really due to decomposing organic matter accumulating in the space, whilst it is frequently a sign of neglect, though common amongst cattle grazing on marshy land.

Treatment.—If convenient, catch the affected sheep, examine the feet, pare away all diseased tissue, wash with antiseptic, and dress with Butter of Antimony.

It is a good plan to keep sheep on a floor covered with lime, or to drive them through a trough containing a solution of Sulphate of Copper.

For foul, dress cattle with antiseptic powder, a pledget of tow, and over all a bandage. Keep feet clean. Carbolic Ointment is useful for this purpose.

FOUNDER OF FEET (*see* Laminitis)

FRACTURES

Fractures of the spinal column, either prove fatal at the time, or subsequently; and the leading symptoms is loss of functional power behind the seat of injury. Fracture of the limbs are frequent, and most of such, in horses, generally necessitate immediate destruction, more especially if below the knee or hock, there being no flesh for support, but when the pastern is split, and the animal a particularly valuable one, three months rest in the slings and the application of a starch bandage may be tried.

The second thigh is often broken in the horse, and, as a rule, it is advisable to destroy the animal at once.

Fracture of the pelvis in the dog is best treated by allowing eight weeks' rest in a confined space; and the animal must be kept entirely undisturbed.

Some pelvic fractures in the horse are curable, others not.

Fracture of the ribs, unaccompanied by a wound in the skin, usually is curable. A fracture may be simple, compound, or comminuted; likewise may be transverse, or oblique, and with or without displacement.

When there is no displacement at the time of fracture, such is spoken of as *deferred*.

When there is a wound, in addition to the

fracture, it complicates matters, but the wound must not be covered with the bandage.

Most of the fractures of the limbs of the dog, are amenable to surgical treatment.

The cardinal signs of fracture are: crepitation, extreme mobility of the part, displacement, swelling, pain and lameness, but any, or all, of the foregoing may be absent, and this is why many of the fractures in the larger animals are so difficult to diagnose.

The sheltered position of a bone, and the mass of muscle covering it, frequently obscure the signs of fracture.

The main principles in management are: to keep back the swelling which can be done by fomenting with hot water; not to disturb the injured parts more than necessary; to prevent the entry of foreign material, if the skin is broken; and to bring the broken ends into apposition, maintaining them in this position — if such be application, by means of suitable bandages, splints, etc.—taking particular care not to apply the bandages too tightly. The average period for repair is about six weeks, but a much longer time, perhaps six months, may be necessary.

G

Gangrene

The term gangrene means mortification, and may be dry or moist. It implies death of the part, and is due to the blood supply being cut off; thus it will follow if a bandage is applied too tightly, or a part constricted by some other means.

Gangrene is not uncommon in the udders of sheep and the teats of cows, occasionally following garget.

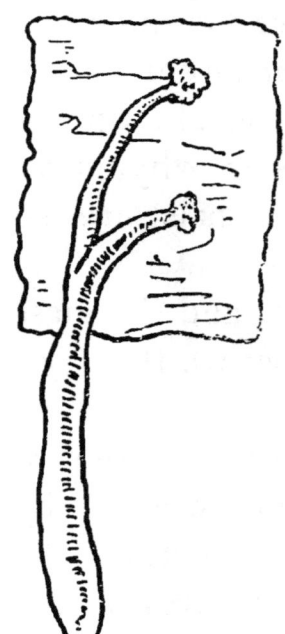

The part becomes cold, greenish, and subsequently black.

In one case, seen by the writer, gangrene of the udder in a cow came on within a few hours. The muscles are sometime gangrenous.

GAPES

So called, owing to the leading symptom, namely gaping. It affects poultry, turkeys, pheasants, partridges and other birds, being produced by minute thread-worms, infecting the air-tubes, and once the disease appears amongst birds it is exceedingly difficult to get rid of, and one infected bird may infect the lot. A wet season favours it, and the worms are coughed up, thus spreading the infection.

MALE AND FEMALE GAPE WORM attached to membrane of windpipe (magnified)

Change the birds to fresh ground, and separate the infected one from the others. See that the water supply is pure, and the addition of a little lime-water will have a beneficial effect.

The affected birds may be caught and a feather

General Management in Disease

dipped in a liniment (composed of 1 part of Terebene to 40 parts of Oil) should be passed down the throat, and then withdrawn.

CHICKEN GAPES

GLANDERS

This is a specific disease, solely caused by minute germs known as the bacilli mallei. It may assume an acute or chronic form, usually the latter, and is essentially an equine disease, but communicable to man, therefore extreme precautions must be used to prevent infection, being a remarkably fatal disease.

The old term "farcy" is not employed now, merely being glanders in which the absorbent vessels, and skin are specially implicated.

Being a notifiable malady, anyone suspecting the

existence of it, must immediately report the matter to the nearest local authority.

Compensation is paid, in Great Britain, for all horses destroyed by order of the local authority.

The clinical features are frequently of a very obscure nature and veterinary surgeons now rely upon the " mallein " test for diagnosis.

In some cases there is a cough; ulceration of the nasal chambers; a discharge from the nose (usually from the left nostril); with or without a knotty swelling, beneath the jaw. But all these signs may be absent, and yet the animal have glanders.

In addition to the foregoing, the skin may show the so-called farcy-buds or buttons, and from these, in due course, an ichorous discharge issues. Isolation is necessary, the disease being incurable.

Grease

This is one of the commonest skin diseases affecting the horse, and it makes its appearance below the hock, between this and the fetlock, and it nearly always affects the hind limbs.

Some cases appear to be constitutional, whereas in others it is a form of parasitic mange, denoted by a greasy condition of the skin, congestion of it; and the hair stands erect, whilst the part emits an offensive odour, chiefly due to the putrefactive discharge.

General Management in Disease

The horse is constantly itching the part, and this leads to thickening, and wrinkling of the skin.

Glossitis (Inflammation of Tongue)

The tongue is sometimes inflamed from external injuries, likewise through specific causes, as actinomycosis (or woody tongue), in which the organ is in a state of chronic inflammation.

Gripes (or Colic)

Pre-eminently this is the commonest disorder affecting the horse, and in rare instances, cattle. It receives different names, such as, fret, belly-ache, the bats, etc., but the term colic should be reserved for pain in the belly arising from functional causes; therefore, one may look upon the following agents as chiefly responsible for colic; Sudden changes of food; drinking excess of water when over-heated; abuse of purgatives; feeding on damaged fodder; excess of green food; presence of worms; lead in the drinking water (lead colic); and other causes, specific and otherwise

When it is accompanied by gas, its gravity is increased, and it is not advisable for an amateur to attempt treatment.

Ordinary cases of colic are denoted by sudden development of pain in the belly—the animal rolling and sweating in proportion to the severity of the attack, which is of variable duration.

Some cases of colic are over within half an hour, whereas others continue for days, but, under these circumstances, the pain is somewhat subdued; and it will generally be found that cases of this nature are due to indigestion, and no relief will follow till the alimentary canal has been cleared with a dose of physic, preferably administered in the form of ball.

It is usual to make an effort to allay the pain, and for this purpose from $\frac{1}{2}$ to 1 oz. of Chlorodyne may be given, or $1\frac{1}{2}$ oz. of Laudanum and 2 oz. of Sulphuric Ether in $\frac{1}{2}$ pt. of water. A clyster may be given and the belly vigorously shampooed, but the writer strongly recommends early veterinary advice.

H

Hæmaturia

This term is applied to the presence of blood in the urine, either as blood, or in a state of solution, and is always a condition of serious illness. (*See* Stone in the Bladder; Red-water, etc.)

Hæmorrhage

Bleeding may occur from a variety of causes, as the result of either external or internal injury; and its gravity is proportionate to the seat of the bleeding.

General Management in Disease

Hæmorrhage from such organs as the lungs; chest; belly; and generative organs, etc., is necessarily of a most dangerous nature; and demands the urgent attention of professional skill.

Bleeding after calving and foaling sometimes occurs, and may lead to a speedy collapse, unless checked at once.

When an artery has been severed and the vessel can be seen, it should be taken up and tied, with a piece of stout thread or silk.

It is a good plan to put two ligatures on, one above and the other below the injury, and then cut the artery between the two.

In other cases a pressure pad may be applied, or the open mouth of the opened vessel touched with a hot iron.

Bleeding from arteries occurs in jets and is of bright scarlet, whereas that from the veins is continuous, and purple.

Cold water is useful for checking bleeding, especially after castration, and sometimes the alternate application of hot and cold water will check it.

Such dirty practices as putting a cob-web on a bleeding part is very liable to infect the wound and must be condemned.

Bleeding from the nose often occurs, more especially in purpura, and demands skilful treatment.

HÆMORRHOIDS (PILES)

This is due to congestion of the veins encircling the anal opening, and frequently observed in the dog, more especially in animals that suffer from constipation, congestion of the liver, etc.

In some cases the vessels begin to bleed (bleeding piles) and the animal aggravates the disease by rubbing the anal opening. Worms predispose to this condition, which is sometimes associated with fistula in the rectum. Give soft food, 10 drops of Sacred Bark every morning, and apply astringent ointment, such as that of Galls.

HEART (AFFECTIONS OF)

All animals are liable to heart troubles—some organic—others functional, but such are beyond recognition by the amateur, and if suspected, necessitate early veterinary advice.

HERNIÆ (*See* Ruptures)

HIP (INJURIES TO)

The hip is sometimes the seat of a bruise or a fracture, the joint being a ball and socket one, and if the fracture is there, the animal must be destroyed.

Fracture of the external angle of the haunch is not uncommon, and is known as "hip-shot,"

General Management in Disease

usually caused by the animal striking the point of the hip against the stable door-post.

The injury is denoted by a flatness and, perhaps, the broken piece of bone may be felt moving about.

Treatment must be left to the veterinary surgeon.

Hocks (Capped)

Capped hock is common enough in the horse, and may or may not constitute an unsoundness. It is the result of a bruise, either continuous or intermittent, and may be of sudden or gradual onset.

When capped hock has just been brought on it is denoted by increased heat in the part; with a slight degree of swelling of the limb; and horses after transit by train, or on board ship, etc., are sometimes found in this condition at the end of the journey.

The skin, bursa, or the bone, may be implicated in capped hock. In most cases it is the skin, and the cellular tissue beneath that is thickened, being commonly produced by bruising the point of the hock against the stall post.

Some horses are night-kickers, but capped hock may be produced through kicking in harness, and likewise during lying or rising, bringing pressure to bear upon the hock.

The swelling varies considerably in size, and one or more hocks may be affected.

In every case it is a blemish.

Hock-joint Open (*See* Joint Open)

Hoven (Dew-Blown) = Tympanitis

This is an exceedingly common complaint, affecting both cattle and sheep—more especially cattle—and the commonest cause, in the case of the last-named, is through a piece of turnip, potato, etc., lodging in the gullet, in other words, choking; but hoven occurs from other causes, such as a sudden change of food, turning out to graze before the dew is off the grass, more especially when the stomach is in an unprepared condition.

A frosted cabbage; turnip; swede; etc., will frequently cause an ox to become hoven.

Hoven sometimes comes on in anthrax, and calves frequently come blown immediately after they have had their milk.

There is a condition known as "chronic" hoven in which cattle blow up immediately after they have been fed, and the author's experience is that such cases are invariably incurable. It arises either through the presence of a foreign body—such as a nail or hair-pin (swallowed), making its exit through the wall of the rumen (paunch) to penetrate the heart, setting up inflammation of the

General Management in Disease

heart-sac, which, sooner or later, proves fatal; but another cause is tuberculosis of the glands (mediastinal) encircling the base of the gullet.

Sometimes these glands are enormously enlarged, and this condition is incurable, so that when an animal is thus affected, the sooner it is slaughtered the better.

Hoven also occurs in the horse, and has been dealt with under the heading of Flatulent Colic.

It is easily known by the drum-like condition of the belly; grunting; and painful breathing.

Unless relieved the animal dies from suffocation, or through rupture of the diaphragm (midriff).

The cause must be removed; purgative medicine given and a bucket of cold water may be thrown over the loins. It is often necessary to puncture, to let out the gas, though this should be avoided if possible, as the animal never thrives quite as well afterwards; but this remark does not apply to the horse. The seat of puncture is in the space between the last rib and the angle of the haunch and on the left side.

Passing the choke-rope (or probang) will sometimes let the gas out of the gullet; but a simple method is to twist a piece of straw into a thick rope, put it inside the mouth, and tie round the horns, so as to act as a mouth gag, and this will often let the gas escape.

Husk or Hoose

This is a parasitical disease affecting calves and lambs, occasionally the pig. It is due to the presence of thread-worms in the air-tubes, there being two species of these worms in sheep, and one in cattle.

The name is derived from the character of the husky cough.

Hoose is most prevalent during damp weather, and marshy lands or low-lying pastures, favour its presence, whilst it readily spreads, the development of the ova being favoured by moisture.

The parasites set up a mechanical bronchitis, and this, in turns, will lead to consolidation of the lungs.

Treatment.—Change to fresh pasturage and house the infected animals. The old remedy consisting of Turpentine, Oil of Tar, and Linseed Oil, say a couple of tablespoonfuls of Linseed Oil, 20 drops of Oil of Tar, and $\frac{1}{4}$ oz. of Turpentine for each calf, daily.

Injections into the trachea, are used by veterinary surgeons.

Fumigation is also employed. Chlorine gas should be avoided.

Treatment had better be left to the Veterinary Surgeon.

A TYPICAL ST. BERNARD

General Management in Disease

I

Indigestion

The term "Indigestion" is chiefly employed for indicating a class of symptoms which arise through perversion of the digestive functions, but, in some cases it is but symptomatic of functional disorder, and in others, organic disease of such organs as the heart, liver, stomach, bowels, etc., is the cause. Treatment accordingly.

In cattle and in horses, likewise sheep and dogs, an accumulation of food in the bowels sometimes provokes dyspeptic symptoms; in fact, colic in the horse is, at times brought on through indigestion.

Worms are a common cause of this affection in dogs.

The terms "stomach staggers," "mad staggers," and "grass staggers" are frequently employed as synonymous with indigestion, and in accordance with the predominating features.

Inflammation of the Bowels (*see* Bowels)

Inflammation of Udder (*see* Mammitis)

Inflammation of Lungs (*see* Pneumonia)

Inflammation of the Eye

All animals are liable to ophthalmia and one or both eyes may be affected. Chemical, mechanical, and specific agencies are the usual causes. The commonest cause in cattle is the presence of a particle of chaff, etc., which excites not only ophthalmia, but opacity of the cornea, and, in some cases, leads to permanent blindness.

In the dog, ophthalmia often occurs during distemper, and the eyeball may be the seat of ulceration. The writer believes that there is a specific or recurrent ophthalmia affecting this animal, which usually produces complete disorganisation of the eye-ball, and is incurable, as a rule.

When the eye-lids are torn, ophthalmia generally follows. If possible remove the cause. Mild cases may be treated with a little Boracic Ointment, or mild yellow Oxide of Mercury Ointment, but when the cornea is cloudy, lead compounds ought not to be used, as such a chemical precipitates the albuminous matter of the cornea. Perhaps the most economical is early Veterinary advice.

ITCH (*see* Mange)

J

JAUNDICE (the Yellows)

Reference has been made to this in connection with distemper, but jaundice as a symptom of deranged liver functions, occurs in all domestic animals, more especially the dog, and unless

General Management in Disease

it is skilfully treated, at the very outset, the chances are that the animal will die.

The jaundiced appearance is due to the entrance of bile pigments into the blood, and their subsequent distribution throughout the body, becoming apparent, as a saffron tint of the skin; whites of the eyes; mucous membranes of the mouth, etc., along with deep yellow colouration of the urine.

When animals are fed on food, too stimulating in its nature, as in the forced feeding of cattle and the horse, congestion of the liver often occurs. The presence of liver flukes in sheep, leads to an allied condition.

Obstruction of the bile ducts; congestion of the liver; exposure to cold; and specific causes are prominent factors in the production of jaundice.

Treatment should be left to veterinary surgeon.

Joint, Open

When a joint has its capsular-ligament penetrated by a puncture, etc., it leads to the discharge of synovia, or joint oil, but a wound in proximity to a joint may, through sloughing, produce open joint. Any joint may be in this condition, but the hock, and the fetlock are those commonly affected. If infection occurs at the time of injury, suppuration sets in, and this complicates matters. If there is disease of bone, blood is frequently intermingled with the joint oil. Open joint is denoted by swelling around the joint, which is hot and painful, causing extreme lameness. Professional treatment is necessary.

K

KIDNEYS (*see* Acute Inflammation of)

L

LAMINITIS (FOUNDER OF THE FEET)

Inflammation of the sensitive laminæ, otherwise termed "fever in the feet," and "founder" is a very common malady in horses, also occasionally observed in cattle. The sensitive laminæ are exceedingly vascular structures and dove-tailed into a horny laminæ on the inner face of the hoof, and as the foot has a rich blood supply it is very liable to congestion, but the worst feature is that there is very little room for the relief of the congestion, consequently the animal suffers most agonizing pain. It assumes acute and sub-acute forms. When a horse has laminitis in all four feet, it is practically, riveted to the ground. As a rule the fore-feet only are implicated. If so, the animal throws them forward, whereas when the hind-ones are affected they are drawn as far under the body. The pulse is quick, oppressed, and hard; the breathing quickened; fever very marked; thirst; bowels constipated; and all the signs that the animal is seriously ill. In some cases the

General Management in Disease

eyelids are swollen, and the hair of the mane and tail is easily pulled out. If the animal is compelled to move, it throws all the weight upon its heels, and shakes from head to foot.

Concussion is one of the commonest causes, but a not infrequent cause is the presence of a particle

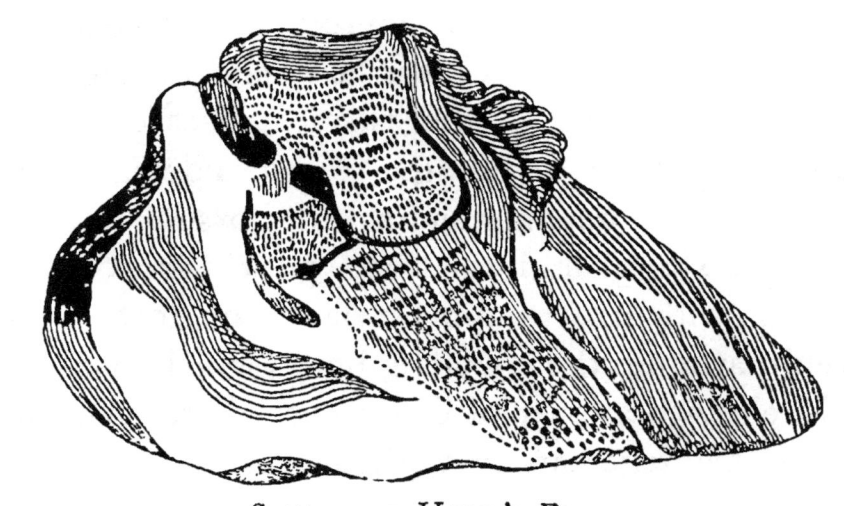

SECTION OF HORSE'S FOOT
Showing the descent of the Coffin bone as the result of Founder or Fever in the Feet.

of decomposing "cleansing" (placenta). This is known as "septic" laminitis and is, generally, much worse than that arising from ordinary causes.

Feeding on wheat and metastases, *i.e.* change of inflammatory action—rank as other causes. In cattle it is generally due to overdriving on hard roads.

Management.—Put animal in the loose-box; feed on green food, or sloppy mashes; have shoes removed, and apply either hot or cold bran poultices to the feet, leaving the rest to the

Veterinary Surgeon, who should be sent for at once.

LARYNGITIS (*see* Sore Throat)

LEGS, SWOLLEN (ŒDEMA)

A swollen limb is merely symptomatic of disease, and as the causes are multifarious, the reader must turn to the various diseases accompanied by such swelling. Mere œdema of the limbs is not uncommon in old horses, or those having a sluggish circulation, and the best way of dealing with it is to apply a layer of cotton wool evenly around the swollen limb (which has been covered with a layer of dry powered starch), and a flannel bandage can be applied over all.

LEG-WEAKNESS IN POULTRY

This is a common ailment to poultry, especially in young birds, and many think that cockerels suffer more than the pullets. It is allied to, but quite distinct from cramp. In that complaint the limbs appear incapable of affording the body proper support, giving way under its weight. The joints are weak, and the condition corresponds to rickets in other animals, though the growth of the body does not remain stunted, as in rickety subjects. It apparently rises through the rapid growth of the body, and defective limb support. Give the best of food; more especially such

General Management in Disease

substances as are rich in Calcium Phosphate. Allow green-bones (crushed); lime and water, and give 5 grains of Phosphate of Lime, in a pill night and morning. Also 20 drops of Cod-Liver Oil daily, along with 20 drops of Parish's Chemical Food.

Lice

All animals are frequently troubled with these pests, and once they make their appearance they are troublesome to get rid of. It is not the lice which are so difficult to destroy, but their eggs. As a rule their presence is a result of neglect, and for their complete eradication all objects that the animal has been in contact with, should be cleansed with boiling water and soda, or given a good coating of gas tar. The best dressing is either a decoction of tobacco or staves-acre seeds, but this must not be too strong. A solution of Quassia may be tried for smaller pets, but one part of paraffin to four parts of milk, so as to afford an emulsion, is a capital remedy, and the animal should be dressed from head to foot with the dressing.

Liver Rot (or Fluke)

Liver rot is very common in sheep, especially those grazing in marshy localities, and when the disease appears, it commonly assumes enzoötic characters, first one sheep, and then another becoming infected. Lambs are predisposed to suffer. Some pastures are famed for the production of it, and as sheep begin to thrive when they are first affected with liver rot, graziers take advantage of this fact, by placing sheep upon it three weeks or so, prior to slaughter. The parasites, evidently, induce an increase of functional power in the liver. Liver rot is due to the presence of fluke-shaped worms, of which there are two species infecting sheep. When mature the liver-fluke is an inch in length, and half an inch in breadth, and of a creamy colour. A single sheep may harbour hundreds of flukes, whilst a single fluke may produce thousands of eggs.

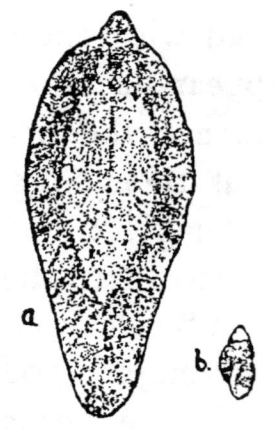

FIG. a.—ADULT LIVER FLUKE
FIG. b.—WATER SNAIL (*Limnaea trunculata*)

The liver-fluke undergoes a remarkable series of changes, after passing out from the body of the sheep with the ejecta.

The ova contained in the decomposing liver-flukes have to pass through a series of changes, before completing their cycle of development.

Briefly put, the embryos pass into ponds, ditches, etc., and become free-swimming by means of minute hair-like processes (cilia), and after a short time the cilia are cast off, and the parasite then penetrates into the lung cavity of the fresh water snail; and after a while goes to some other part of the snail, such as the liver, and whilst within the nurse, other generations are formed, and subsequently the parasite leaves the nurse, and develops a snow-white cyst which adheres to particles of grass, etc., and in this form may be consumed by sheep. The cyst wall is then dissolved in the bowel, and, by means not well understood, gains access to the bile ducts and gall bladder, producing the well known symptoms of liver rot, which are: gradual loss of flesh; clapping of the wool; the wool falling out; the back becomes hollow; eyes yellowish; and in due course the belly becomes pendulous owing to dropsy. The presence of liver-flukes in the ejecta is positive evidence of the disease, which seldom prevails on salt marshes, and this is one reason why sheep raisers send their flock towards the coast when liver rot appears. Change to upland pasturage. Separate infected sheep, and give Salt and Sulphate of Iron in food; say 1 teaspoonful of Salt and 40 grains of powdered Sulphate of Iron to each sheep daily.

LOCK-JAW (TETANUS)

Lock-jaw is one of the most fatal maladies affecting the horse, and is solely due to the bacilli tetani, which are exceedingly minute organisms, shaped like a drum-stick, and having a spore at one end. A remarkable feature is the presence of these germs in garden soil, and it would appear that they are present more in some localities than others, because some practitioners hardly ever see a case of this disease, whereas others are constantly having such cases. The germs do not enter the circulation, but excrete their poisonous products (tetanine) from the wound where they remain, and which constitutes their portal of entry.

Castration is occasionally followed by tetanus, so are wounds in the feet, and sometimes saddle-galls; or even the insertion of a seton.

The leading symptoms are muscular spasms, as the disease develops; but quite early on if the animal is touched under the chin suddenly, the winking membranes are shot across the eyes, which is pathognomic. The spasms increase in severity; and the slightest noise brings them on, rendering the animal convulsed, from head to foot. In some cases the jaws are locked, and this is frequent in the horse. Internal temperature is often very high, and sweating in patches frequent. Breathing is embarrassed, and the facial expression anxious, whilst the bowels are usually confined. Death commonly occurs within a few days,—and, during convalescence, relapses are frequent. In a case of this character, the animal must be kept under lock and key, so as not to be disturbed, and veterinary advice should at once be obtained.

LYMPHANGITIS (*see* Weed)

KERRY COW

General Management in Disease

M

MAGGOTS IN SHEEP (*see* Wounds)

MAMMITIS (*see* Udder)

MANGE

Mange is a common affection especially in horses, sheep, dogs, and cats, constituting in the sheep, "Sheep Scab," which is a notifiable disease, and so, in some localities, is mange in the horse. There are 3 species of parasites, but the commonest are the Sarcoptes Acari; producing Sarcoptic Mange. All forms of parasitic mange are communicable, either to the same, or different species of animals. Mange parasites live upon the superficial parts of the skin and it is the female acari that do so much damage.

In the dog there is the so-called "follicular," or "black mange,"—a most intractable form of mange. The terms "Red Mange," "Blotch" etc., are indiscriminately applied to both parasitic mange and other skin affections, of a non-parasitic nature. The chief signs of mange are: falling off of the hair, or wool; redness and vesiculation of the skin; at first in patches which, if neglected, become confluent. These patches appear upon the back; beneath the mane; on the neck; and at the root of the tail; and sometimes upon the limbs, depending on the species of parasite. In sheep-scab the back and the breast are the commonest situations at the onset, but, of course, any part

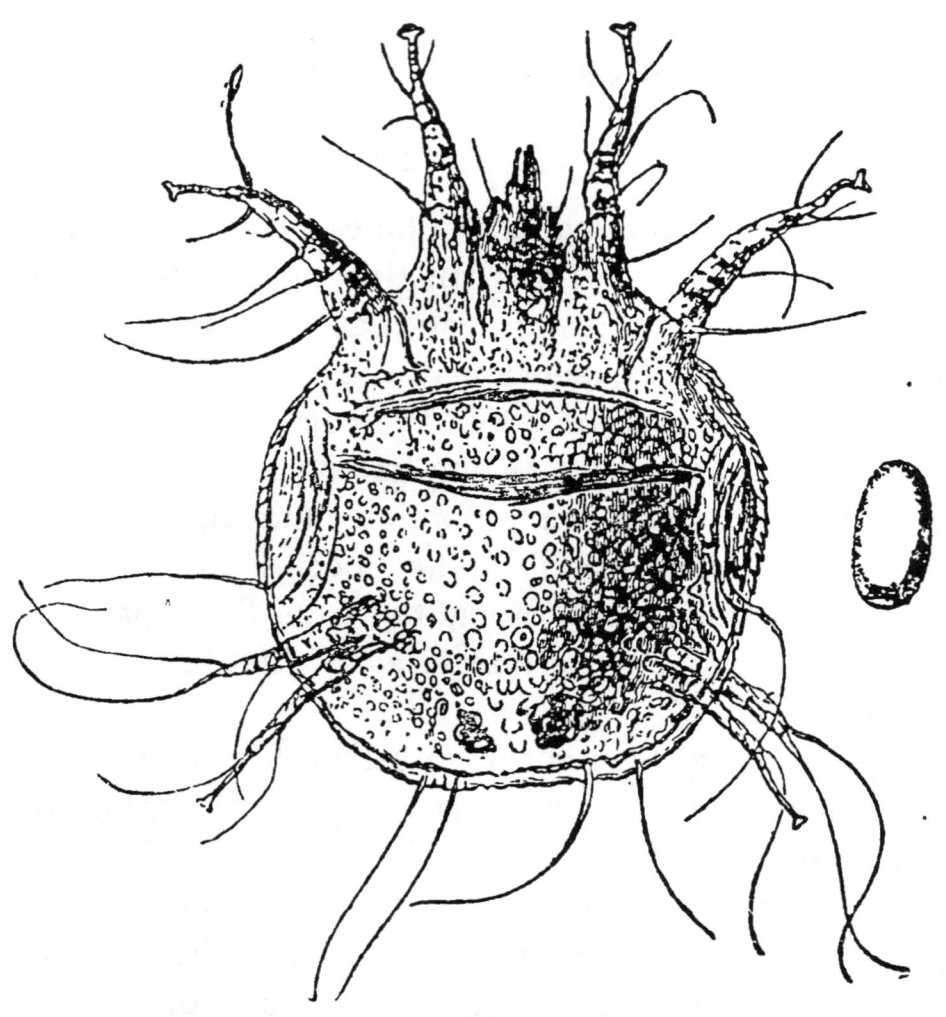

SHEEP SCAB MITE (enlarged)

may be affected. If the skin is "itched" with the fingers, the sheep manifest appreciation by standing quiet meanwhile. Rubbing, scratching and biting the parts, are common signs of mange in all animals.

General Management in Disease

The discharge from the sores dries upon the surface, forming scabs or crusts.

Management.—Compulsory dipping is now

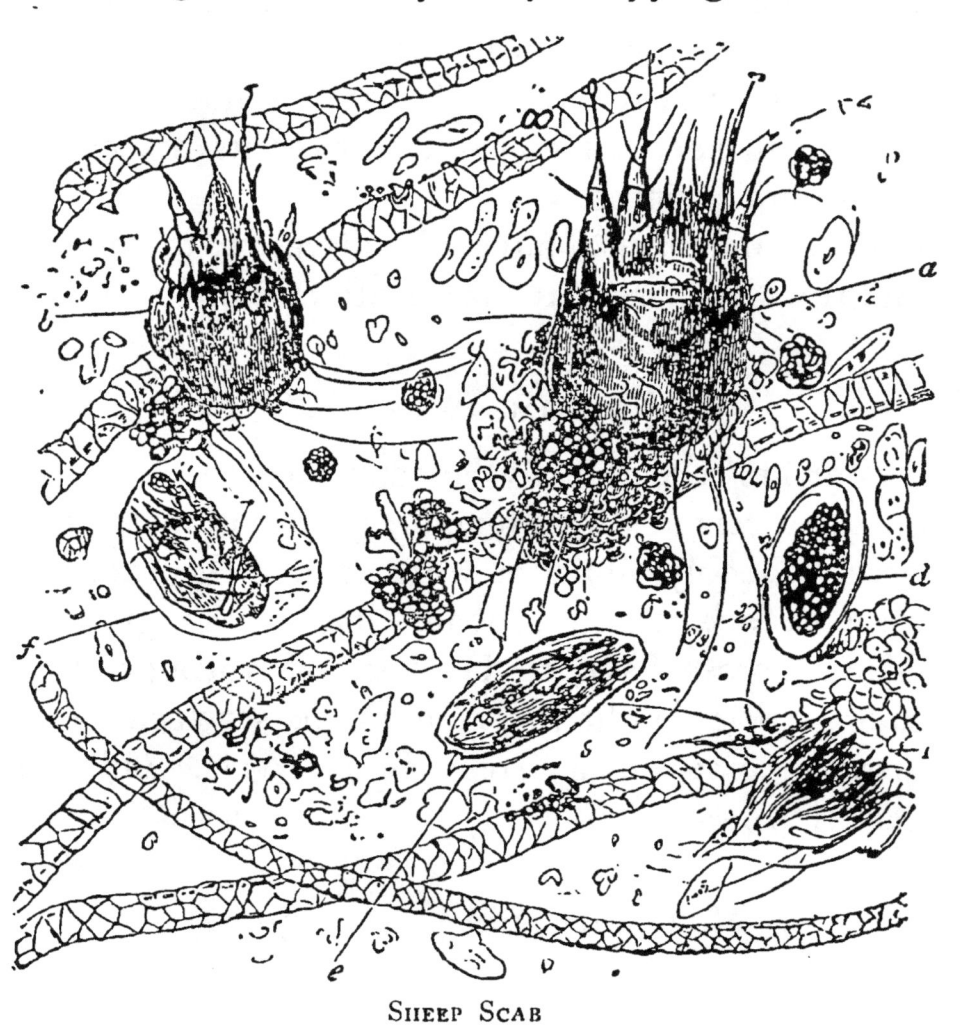

SHEEP SCAB

necessary in the case of sheep, and for horses and dogs a useful liniment consists of 2 oz. of Oil of Tar, 4 oz. of Flowers of Sulphur, and 1 pt. of some common oil—Rape or Colza—rubbed well into the diseased parts; but before doing so, wash with soft soap and warm water, reapplying every fourth day, till disease is cured. In some cases it is advisable to clip off the whole of hair, and dress from head to foot with liniment.

The recurrent nature of mange renders it expedient to keep an animal free from its associates for several months.

Cats, sometimes, convey the disease to the horse, and the attendant may also contract itch.

MEGRIMS (VERTIGO)

Vertigo occasionally affects the horse. The animal is seized with a temporary loss of consciousness, probably whilst at work, and if the attack is a severe one it will probably fall to the ground. Many horses have to be cast off through this failing, being unfit for responsible service. The attacks come on at irregular intervals, and the causes are obscure.

MORTIFICATION (see Gangrene)

MOULTING

Most fowls moult or cast their feathers during Autumn, or else at the close of the Summer. Winter layers generally begin to moult in the Summer. In the moulting season it is a good plan to keep the cock and hen birds separate, which favours better plumage.

General Management in Disease

Birds must be liberally fed at this period, and the following foods will be found as suitable as aught that can be given.

Lean Meat, Oats, Beans, Peas, Rice, and green food. Keep in a warm house, and on dry ground.

N

Navicular Disease

This disease is very common amongst the lighter breeds of horses, and it affects the forefeet only. It is known under the popular title of "Grogginess," and such an animal as a Grog—terms derived from peculiarity of action, arising through the existence of this disease, which affects the cartilage of the navicular bone: the navicular bone itself, the bursa (or lubricating sheath) and the flexor tendon where it passes over the bone. Any, or all, of the foregoing structures may be implicated. Navicular disease is incurable, and progressive, rendering the animal of no commercial value, but not completely destroying its utility; as a horse, thus affected, may continue to work on soft ground, whilst a considerable percentage of cab-horses, working in towns, are affected with it. The short cat-like step, together with the upright fetlock, and lameness immediately the animal comes from the stable, are the most characteristic signs. Excision of a portion of the nerve supplying the foot with sensation, is practised, in order to remove the lameness.

Navel Ill

The navel is the seat of disease in this complaint, being the point of infection and, from this focus other troubles arise, such as, joint-ill, scour, etc.

The navel becomes swollen and reddened, and, in some cases, urine issues from the opening. It occurs in foals, dogs, calves and lambs; but the complications of a rheumatoid nature do not occur in the dog.

The disease spreads along the track of the cord, and death may occur within a few days, hence the necessity for due regard, at, or about the time of birth, to cleanliness. Dust the part with a little Boracic Acid Powder, or smear with Carbolic Oil, etc.

Ophthalmia (*see* Inflammation of Eye)

Over-reach

This is an injury produced by the sharp edge of the inner rim of the hind shoe close to the toe striking the fetlock joint or the heel in the forefoot. The wound is usually a flap of skin, which should be cut off, in order to bring about speedy healing, or union of parts.

General Management in Disease

Apply a linseed poultice for 2 or 3 days, and then dress with an antiseptic, or Carbolic Oil, etc.

P

Paralysis

Any organ, or portion of the body, may be in a paralytic condition, the paralysis representing a loss of functional power, and such loss may be either temporary or permanent. Paralysis of the body may be complete or partial, and affect the right or left side. When a bone in the limb is fractured the part below the seat of the injury is in a temporary state of paralysis. Again in Amaurosis (or glass eye) the eye is paralytic. Internal organs, such as the bowels, bladder, larynx, etc., are not uncommonly paralytic. Paralysis arising from injuries to the spinal cord is usually incurable, and the same remark is applicable to morbid growths pressing upon the nerves. Paralysis of the tongue is not uncommon in the horse and is incurable, whilst facial paralysis, affecting one or both sides varies in its termination. Paralysis frequently occurs in cows before or after calving, likewise in dogs at, or about the time of distemper. It is sometimes brought about by constipation in which case a purgative, or enema, should be administered. Treatment necessarily varies in accordance with the cause.

PARASITES, INTERNAL, IN SHEEP (*see* WORMS)

PARTURIENT APOPLEXY (MILK FEVER)

Parturient apoplexy, or dropping after calving, is a disease entirely confined to cows, and heavy milkers seem to be predisposed to this affection, hence the reason why such breeds as the Alderney; Ayrshire; Shorthorn, etc., are so frequently affected with this complaint, which is particularly prevalent in dairying districts. At one time enormous losses were caused by it, in fact it might not have been inaptly termed the "Dairyman's Scourge," but since the introduction of Schmit's treatment the losses have been reduced to five per cent. or thereabouts; when death occurs in the present day, it is either due to some complication such as pneumonia, etc., or else improper treatment, because the old fashioned treatment is not the slightest use in this complaint, and it only carried with it one economical recommendation as a set off, and that was, the advisability for slaughter, in preference to its adoption. Although termed "Milk Fever" there is no fever, the temperature being practically normal. The term "dropping after calving" is frequently used, but does not necessarily imply that the animal has parturient apoplexy, in fact a considerable per centage of cows drop within about 43 hours of calving, yet never pass into the stages of this malady; hence

General Management in Disease

the reason why many got the credit for the cure of an animal merely affected with "post-partum" paralysis. Some cows drop before calving—"Ante-partum" paralysis. It is seldom that parturient apoplexy comes on before the second or third calf, and generally, within 48 hours from delivery. Denoted by a staggering gait; uneasiness, followed by a gradual loss of control over movements; and difficulty in rising, more especially the uplifting of the hind quarters. In the course of a few hours, the animal is unable to get up, though it may make repeated attempts. In due course the head is turned towards the breast, and loss of consciousness frequently follows, whilst the excretory organs are in abeyance. Unless the animal is properly treated, death inevitably supervenes.

Management.—Put cow in a deep bed of straw and in a clean place. Pack up with boltens of straw, so that she rests upon her breast and not upon her side; taking particular care to have the head raised well up by packing with straw. Send for the Veterinary Surgeon at once.

PERITONITIS (*see* Inflammation of Bowels)

PILES (*see* Haemorrhoids)

PLEURISY

The term pleurisy is expressive of inflammation of the serous membrane of the lungs, and is a common enough disease, being frequently associated with pneumonia. It may arise from external injuries, such as a penetrating wound of the chest, but is generally part and parcel of some complaint such as influenza, distemper, etc. Exposure to cold appears to be a cause. The worst features about it is the tendency towards effusion, and when this is excessive, especially if the animal's constitution is weak, the chances of recovery are small. In the early stages, horses grunt sometimes when compelled to move. Internal temperature rises several degrees: the pulse becomes hard and wiry, and auscultation reveals friction murmur. Treatment should be left to Veterinary Surgeon.

PNEUMONIA

Inflammation of the lungs is of frequent occurrence in all animals, and there is an infectious form of this disease in the horse. At one time the stock-owners of Great Britain were troubled with contagious pneumonia or lung fever in cattle, but fortunately this does not exist in the British Isles. Lung inflammation is generally associated with pleurisy, and is often brought on through bronchitis, which produces what is known

General Management in Disease

as catarrhal pneumonia, in contra-distinction to another form, termed "Lobar," in which there are three distinct stages, viz.: 1st, engorgement; 2nd, red hepatization; 3rd, grey hepatization or red and grey solidification. In distemper, and influenza, lung complications are frequent, and many deaths are attributable to this disease. Counter irritants, such as mustard, should be applied externally. The animal well clothed and kept warm. It is a disease demanding professional attendance.

POISONING

Arsenical poisoning has been dealt with in its proper place, and much the same treatment is applicable to antimony. Strychnine poisoning is not uncommon in the dog, and is denoted by a series of rapid muscular contractions, which convulse the animal from head to foot.

Yew poisoning occasionally occurs in the horse, and death supervenes very rapidly. Carbolic acid poisoning sometimes arises in the dog, through absorption of the drug, more especially if hot water be used for washing the animal with strong carbolic soap. When the poison is an acid give an alkali: if an alkali give an acid. Lead poisoning in cattle should be treated with Epsom Salts, and dilute Sulphuric Acid (*see also* Belladonna).

Prolapsus Uteri (Falling of Womb)

also

Prolapsus Ani, &c.

Inversion or prolapse of the womb is not an uncommon accident, especially in cows, sheep and sows; more generally occurs after delivery. Previous prolapse is a predisposing cause, but violent straining of any kind, combined with loss of tone in the parts, favours its occurrence. If the "cleansing" has not been expelled, this will be found attached, and must be removed before the organ is replaced. When the womb hangs out for a few hours it becomes engorged and gangrene sets in, therefore the return of the organ is quite useless, demanding amputation. Sometimes fatal bleeding happens at the time of prolapse. Professional aid is absolutely indispensable, but meanwhile a couple of assistants should support the organ in a sheet, using some mild antiseptic dissolved in warm water, so as to keep it clean. Prolapse of the anus is a troublesome accident, and not uncommon in dogs. It is denoted by a sausage like projection behind, arising through excessive straining, and an atonic condition of the part.

Prolapse of the vagina is denoted by a tumour-like swelling, bright red in colour, protruding between the lips of the vulva, particularly seen

General Management in Disease

when cattle are laid down. The application of a truss is useful in such cases.

PSORIASIS (*see* Eczema)

PYÆMIA (*see* Blood Poisoning)

R

RABIES

This is essentially a canine scourge, but fortunately is absent ftom the British Isles, and the quarantine regulations afford the best preventive against its re-introduction. With the cessation of rabies, hydrophobia has necessarily ceased also, thanks to the Muzzling Order.

Rabies is, unquestionably, a specific disease and communicable by inoculation only, from dog to dog, and from this animal, and the wolf, fox, etc., to the horse and other animals, whilst man may suffer from hydrophobia, through being bitten by a rabid animal. Is constantly found in certain countries, such as India, Burmah, Russia, etc. Is a very ancient malady, and its deadly nature was known to earliest observers. It assumes both "furious" and "dumb" forms. In the "dumb" form, the lower jaw is paralytic, whilst in the "furious" form, the animal gradually alters in its temperament; snaps at imaginary objects; has a disposition to wander; seeking seclusion; biting any objects confronting it. Although thirsty, it is unable to swallow, owing to extreme congestion of the throat. The bark becomes altered, and, once heard, is easily recognised again. In addition to the foregoing, the animal bites at the seat of inoculation, and attempts to swallow particles of foreign matter, such as hay, straw and so forth. Delirium and paralysis subsequently set in, followed by death. The average duration of the disease is about six days, whilst the period of incubation varies, but, as a rule, is about six weeks, though in some cases, six months.

RED-WATER AND BLACK-WATER

This is a disorder affecting cattle and sheep, more especially the former, chiefly young stock, but there is a form of red-water which may come on three weeks after calving and is called Parturient red-water, being a much more serious malady than this affection in the young. Recent investigations have shown that red-water is due to a species of protozöa (minute organisms), which assume a whip-like form. These invade the blood-cells, causing the discharge of the colouring matter, which passes off in the urine. These organisms are said to be introduced into the blood through the medium of the Cattle Tick, producing what is known as "piro-plasmosis." At one time, it was thought to be due to acrid herbs and impoverished fodder. The symptoms are: a reddish-tinted urine, which gradually deepens, assuming the colour of port wine, and owing to the black character of it, it is frequently spoken of as "Black-Water." Sometimes there is diarrhœa, and sometimes constipation. The former is a salutary process, in this complaint. To cows, no matter whether purged or not, a good dose of purgative must be given; followed up by Sulphate of Iron, with plenty of eggs, milk and whisky.

Rheumatism, Chest Founder, or Kennel Lameness

Rheumatism assumes both acute and chronic forms and may attack either a joint or the muscles. The precise cause is unknown, but a hyper-acidity of the blood is one theory as to its causation, and micro-organisms is another. Muscular rheumatism is not common in the horse, the writer has only seen one typical case, but in dogs it is fairly common. Kennelmen are familiar with it, as an affection of the chest muscles, hence the use of the term "chest founder." It is not always that the disease is confined to this part of the dog, because the loins may be affected (lumbago); whereas in other instances most of the muscles are affected. It is quite possible that many diseases affecting the bones and joints in the horse are of a rheumatic nature, more especially the deposits of new bony material in the regions of the hock and fetlock joints. A damp kennel favours rheumatism, which is a troublesome disease amongst sporting dogs, in particular.

Treatment.—Keep animals in a warm house; feed on soft food; give a dose of purgative medicine, and rub the joints with Capsicum's Liniment, or White Oil, night and morning. If chronic, for dog, give 5 grs. of Iodide of Potash, twice daily, and 30 grs. of this for the horse in a little water. Acute rheumatism is accompanied by fever; and there is a disease known as rheumatoid arthritis or joint-ill, which simulates rheumatism, but is, in reality, an infection arising from the umbilical cord.

Ribs (*see* Fractures)

Rickets

This is a disease chiefly affecting the dog, and is due to defective assimilation. The growth becomes stunted: the bones abnormal: the joints enlarged: and the animal arrives at the adult stage in a deformed condition. The long bones do not increase in length, and their extreme flexibility appears to be due to a deficiency of mineral matter in them.

Give cod-liver oil: extract of malt: Fellows'

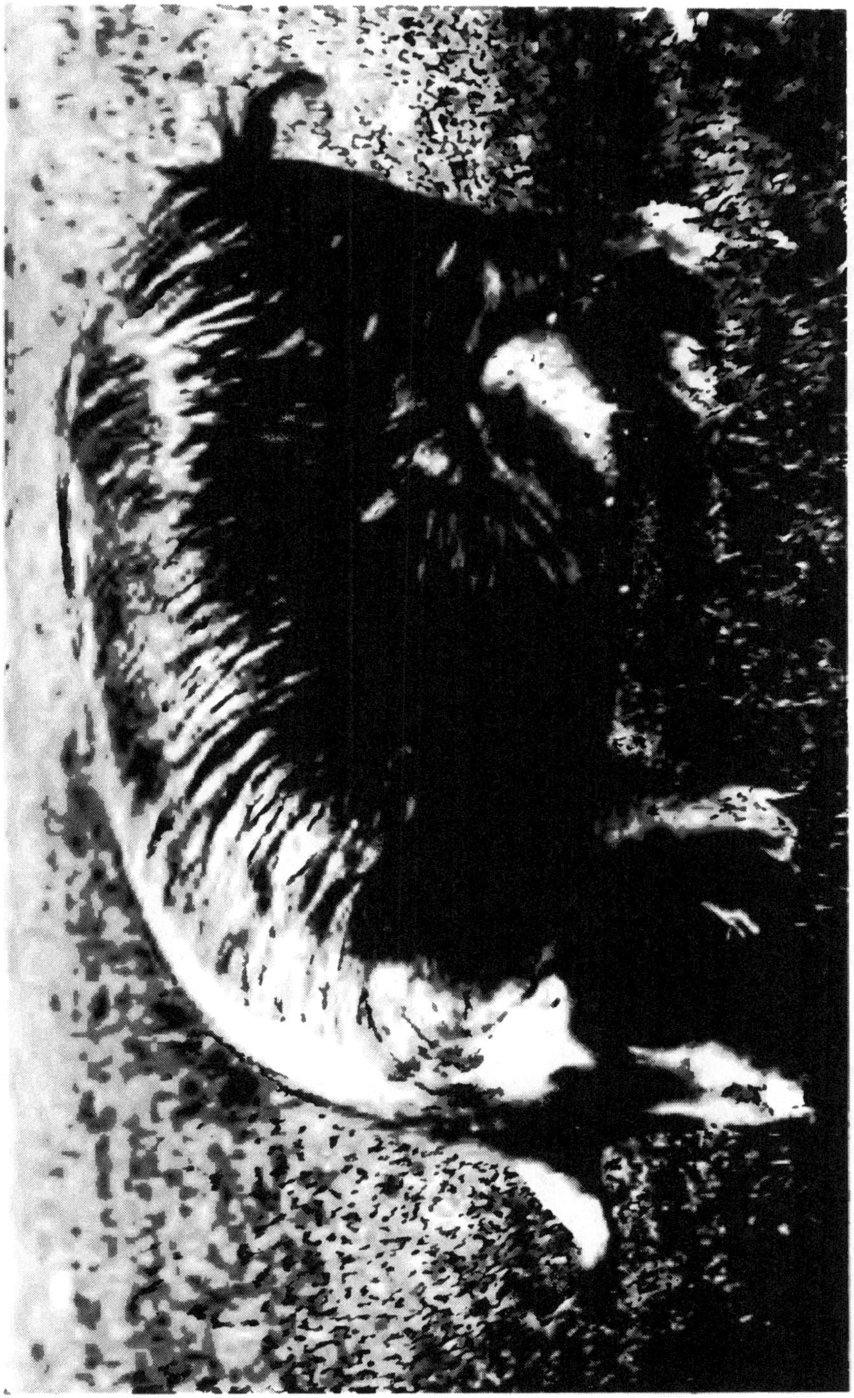

General Management in Disease

Syrup of Hypophosphites and Lime Water; along with an abundance of nourishing food.

RINDERPEST (OR CATTLE PLAGUE, MURRAIN)

Fortunately for Great Britain this disease has ceased to exist in our Islands, although it is constantly present in certain other countries, such as Russia, etc. The recent outbreak in South Africa caused enormous losses, but preventative treatment has now been found.

RINGWORM

This is a common disease amongst calves, and man may contract it from this source. The horse, dog and cat are sometimes affected. There are two varieties of the disease, and it is due to a vegetable fungus infesting the shafts and roots of the hairs. Filthy surroundings favour the disease.

Dress the patches with Iodine Ointment, or a little Mercurial Ointment. Whitewash the byres, stables, etc.

RING-BONE

Ring-bone is a very common affection of the pastern-joint of the horse, either of the fore- or hind-limbs. It is spoken of as "high" or "low," in accordance with its position;—likewise as "true" or "false," but the absurdity of the last two names is evident. Commonly the deposit of new bone is situate just above the coronet, and often assumes the form of a ring, hence the name. It may be situate on the front or hind face of the bone, and the new bony deposit represents Nature's method of strengthening the part, but in ring-bone, lameness frequently exists during the formative stage, and may persist after the acute inflammatory signs have subsided. The pastern-joint or fellock-joints are sometimes fused together, through the inflammatory products. Both heavy and light horses are liable to ring-bone, and the lameness arising therefrom is generally incurable. It constitutes unsoundness, and the commercial value of the animal with such, is small.

Roaring

Roaring is a sound symptomatic of disease, either of a temporary or permanent character, usually the latter. The sound may be emitted either during slight or severe exertion, depending upon the degree of diseased activity. Many believe that roaring is hereditary, but this is open to doubt, there being much evidence both pro and con.

A horse may be passed as sound one hour, and develop roaring the next, because its causes are variable. It must be admitted that in fully 85 per cent of cases the roaring sound is due to degenerative changes in certain muscles of the

General Management in Disease

larynx, which undergo fatty degeneration, but whether the fatty degeneration is primary or secondary is open to doubt. The recurrent nerve is implicated, as it supplies motor power to the muscles of the larynx. A morbid growth in the nasal chamber, such as a bony tumour (or a polypus), sometimes causes continuous roaring, whilst a stalked tumour growing in juxta-position to the larynx, may pass over the glottal opening, occlude it, and produce the roaring sound. With an alteration in the position of the growth, the sound may disappear. Lead-poisoning, and a species of Indian Vetch occasionally produce a similar sound. In short, mechanical obstructions in any part of the air-tube, may give rise to roaring.

Strangles, in exceptional cases, is succeeded by roaring.

A roarer is of slight commerical value, there being no cure for it (if due to disease of the laryngeal muscles), but many horses continue to do useful work with a tube in their throat.

RUPTURES

A rupture consists of the displacement of an organ, or tissue from its normal position. The commonest rupture in the horse is at the navel, and is called "Umbilical." This animal sometimes suffers from "*scrotal*" rupture, in which a portion of the bowel descends from the belly down the inguinal canal into the scrotum, sometimes to such an extent that several feet are hanging down behind. The chief danger in connection with ruptures in this region is their tendency to become strangulated, and horses are occasionally coliced from this cause.

Treatment purely surgical. There are numerous other ruptures (*see* also Prolapsus Uteri, etc).

ROUP

is a disease affecting poultry and allied to distemper in the dog. Its highly infective nature is good evidence that it is a specific disease, and when it appears in the poultry-yard is most difficult to eradicate. It is spread by means of feeding utensils, food, drinking water, etc., also by birds. It is very infectious, and when runs have become fouled with this disease, the best plan is to let them lie fallow. Apply hot gas lime, or salt, and plough up; or the ground may be trenched. Isolate the infected birds. The leading features are: a creamy discharge from the nose and eyes, which thickens, and occludes the nasal and occular cavities, and may cause suffocation. The birds drop their wings, mope and sneeze, and in this manner infect other birds. It may easily be introduced by recently purchased birds, hence the advisability of keeping such

General Management in Disease

separate for about a month. To each give ¼ gr. of powered Capsicums, combined with ⅛ gr. of Carbonate of Ammonia and a drop of Oil of Eucalyptus made into a pill, and given night and morning. Sponge eyes and nose with a little Boro-glycerine. Throughly wash and disinfect every utensil; and house, etc. Attendants may spread the disease.

S

Sand Crack

Sand crack implies a splitting of the wall of the hoof, beginning at the coronet, and commonly situate at the inner quarter, if at fore-feet, and at the toe in the hind ones. It is due to an imperfect secretion of the horny fibres; and not an uncommon cause of lameness, but such lameness arises when the sensitive structures on the face of the pedal bone get nipped between the edges of the crack. May begin on the inner or the outer side of hoof, and constitutes unsoundness.

False quarter predisposes to sand crack. The best plan is to throw the animal off work, and draw a line, transversely, below the crack. If the crack causes lameness, it may be clasped, special sand-cracks bolts being sold for this purpose. Take the pressure off the wall by cutting a notch below the crack, or seating out the shoe below the crack.

SCABIES AND SHEEP SCAB (*see* Mange)

SCOUR (*see* Acute Scour, also Diarrhoea)

SORE THROAT

This arises from a variety of causes; thus, for instance, it is common in horses when they have influenza, and is denoted by a cough, hard at first, and subsequently becoming moist. The moist nature of the cough usually becoming evident when there is a free discharge from the nose. The animal has a difficulty in swallowing; liquid sometimes coming down from the nostrils. Fever is generally present, together with other signs of ill-health.

Treatment. Keep the animal warm; rub throat with some stimulating linament, or with mustard paste; give linseed gruel, scalded oats, and bran as food. To drinking water add $\frac{1}{2}$ ounce Chlorate of Potash, night and morning.

STAGGERS

So called owing to the staggering gait. The terms "mad," "grass" and "sleepy staggers" are often employed, and have been referred to under the heading of indigestion (which see).

STIFF JOINT (*see* Anchylosis)

General Management in Disease

SIDE-BONE

This is an extremely common disease, more especially in cart-horses; in fact, a very large proportion of these animals have side-bone, which, however, does not necessarily produce lameness. The cartilages affected in this disease comprise two lateral plates, situate on either side of the hoof, each plate being attached to the upper and back part of the wings of the coffin-bone, and projecting at the back of the hoof, in a line with the coronet. The cartilages can be felt, yielding like a piece of elastic when pressed with the thumb if healthy, but when affected with side-bone, the springy feel is lost. The change is really one of calcification of the cartilages, and the disease affects one or both fore-feet, either at the inner, or outer side of the foot. When lameness is present it is due to pressure upon the soft structures. The size of side-bone is no criterion as regards lameness. It constitutes unsoundness, and there should be a reduction in the price, but not much, if the feet are good and strong; the heels well open; the animal five years, of a heavy breed, and free from lameness.

SPLINT

The term splint is applied to a small, though variable sized, bony deposit, situated upon the back or side of the canon-bone. All classes of horses are liable to splint, but such is more detrimental in animals required for fast work. The splinty deposit represents the legacy of an acute inflammation of the bone-skin at the seat of the splint, in fact constitutes nature's method of repair, at the seat of injury.

A splint may be *simple* or compound. In the former, there is a solitary deposit of new bone, whereas in the latter several deposits (splints), which are commonly more or less connected together, forming an irregular chain between the large and small splint bones. The size of the splint does not necessarily bear any relationship to the degree, and duration of, lameness. When a splint is situated close beneath the knee, it is very liable to give rise to persistent lameness, and Veterinary Surgeons have agreed that such should always be a cause of rejection, when examining the soundness. All forms of splint really constitute unsoundness, and the presence of it ought to bring about the abatement (say £5) of price. Lameness is more liable to arise in young horses than in the case of seasoned ones.

The chief cause of splint is concussion; sprain, and external injury, such as a blow, etc., on the canon-bone. Many believe it to be hereditary. Lameness is often present whilst the splint is being formed. Splint sometimes disappears spontaneously. If necessary the deposit can be removed by opera-

General Management in Disease

tion. Blistering, rest and point firing, constitute the best methods of dealing with splint. In the formative stage, use cooling applications.

STRANGLES
Showing the Swelling under the Jaw

STRANGLES

Strangles is a very common malady, and most young horses have an attack of it, but it is not uncommon in the aged. It is, no doubt, a specific complaint, and transmitted from one horse to another by direct and, probably, indirect means. It assumes regular and irregular forms. Regular when the abscess is situated beneath the jaw or at the point of the shoulder; but "irregular" when removed from this situation, or appearing internally. In its simple form, it is a benign complaint, but when irregular frequently the cause of death. There is, generally, a slight degree of fever; soreness of the throat; difficulty in swallowing; a cough, which is hard at first, subsequently becoming moist when the discharge issues freely from the nose. The abscess that forms between the branches of the lower jaw sometimes occupies several weeks before it reaches maturity, which is favoured by blistering it. As soon as ripe, it requires opening. Very often abscesses form all down the neck and hinder restoration to health. Send for Veterinary Surgeon. Keep animals warm and isolate.

Sturdy (Turn-sick or Gid)

The term sturdy is applied to a disease affecting sheep, indicated by such symptoms as turning round in a circle: dizziness: jumping up: partial blindness. It is due to a bladder worm or hydatid (coenurus cerebralis) locating itself upon some portion of the brain (either the cerebellum or cerebrum), and represents the

DEVONSHIRE LONG WOOL EWES

General Management in Disease

larval form of a tape-worm, resident in the bowel of the dog, known as "Taenia coenurus." Sheep acquire this disease through drinking infected water, or grazing upon infected land: hence the advisability of keeping shepherds' dogs free from tape-worm. In addition to the symptoms of vertigo, the cranial-bone, over the seat of the hydatid, sometimes undergoes softening, and shepherds very often remove the hydatid, there being special instruments for this purpose. The fluid and wall of the cyst must both be extracted. The small white bodies in the fluid represent the heads of future tape-worms, and must, therefore, be destroyed. The best method of dealing with a sheep so affected is to slaughter.

SWELLED LEGS (*see* Legs Swollen)

SWINE FEVER

Swine fever, also known as swine plague, is, unfortunately, for pig breeders of this and other countries, far to common; and, in spite of the stringent regulations adopted by the Board of Agriculture, it continues to be remarkably prevalent.

It is a specific disease allied to enteric in man, without, in many cases, sufficient clinical phenomena to render the diagnosis certain; hence the reason why the Veterinary Inspectors have so frequently to make one or more post-mortems before a definite opinion can be formed; moreover, confirmation of the opinion rests with the Board of Agriculture, as this is a notifiable disease, and compensation is paid out of the funds of the local authority, acting under the directions of the Board of Agriculture, and anyone suspecting the existence of it on their premises should notify it at once, otherwise much inconvenience may be caused. It is an infectious complaint, and communicable through drinking-vessels and feeding-troughs, etc., to other pigs, but not to other animals so far as known.

T

Teats (Soreness of)

The teats of cows are frequently sore, such soreness arising from several causes. Warty growths upon them are common, and frequently lead to bleeding, so that when the teats are handled the animals object to being milked.

Cracks, or fissures, are also common, and are chiefly the result of allowing the teats to become wet and foul. There is a specific inflammation, which shows itself as an eruption upon the teats. This is the so-called "cow-pox," and is transmissible from one cow to another, by the hands of the milker.

Circular ulcers follow the blisters, and very

angry looking sores are formed, which sometimes lead to a septic form of garget.

Dress with Peruvian Balsam Ointment, or Boroglycerine.

Absolute cleanliness needful.

Teats Impervious

Sometimes the duct of the teat becomes closed. If so this will require surgical measures for relief. The passage of the teat syphon requires great care, otherwise more harm than good will be done.

Tetanus (*see* Lock-Jaw)

Tuberculosis (Consumption)

Tuberculosis, commonly known under the title of grapes, ulcers, etc., is an exceedingly common disease in cattle and poultry, but occurs in other animals, such as the horse, dog and cat, though less frequently. Probably fully 30 per cent. of cattle are affected with it. It is a specific, infectious disease, due to Koch's bacillus, and its presence in cattle constitutes one of the most serious drawbacks, not only from a butcher's point of view, but also from a dairyman's. It assumes acute and chronic forms, but chronic tuberculosis may at any time become acute; and, when it does so, the animal rapidly succumbs. In animals it is usually in the chronic form. Many instances have been given of poultry acquiring the disease from man through devouring tubercular sputum, whilst the writer has frequently seen cats gradually die from the disease after feeding upon the bodies of tuberculous fowls.

It is thought by some authorities that the milk of cattle is only infective when the udder is the seat of tubercular disease, but tubercular garget in cattle is not a common complaint. Tuberculosis in cattle usually assumes the form of nodular new growths adherent to the pulmonary and intercostal pleurae, and these growths have a grapey appearance. The pleural membrane on the chest wall, and that reflected over the midriff, is sometimes one mass of these growths; whilst the lungs have tubercles of variable size and grapy outgrowths therefrom.

When the disease is generalised, the pericardium, liver, kidneys, uterus, vagina, larynx and trachea may be implicated.

The glands of the bowels, lungs, and other lymphatics, especially those in the region of the shoulder and thigh, are generally affected, and such appear to be the tracks of infection.

It is believed that tuberculosis is communicable, both by ingestion and inhalation. In poultry, the liver is commonly the seat of the disease, whilst large calcareous tumours occur in the belly.

In the horse the spleen (or melt) is the principal

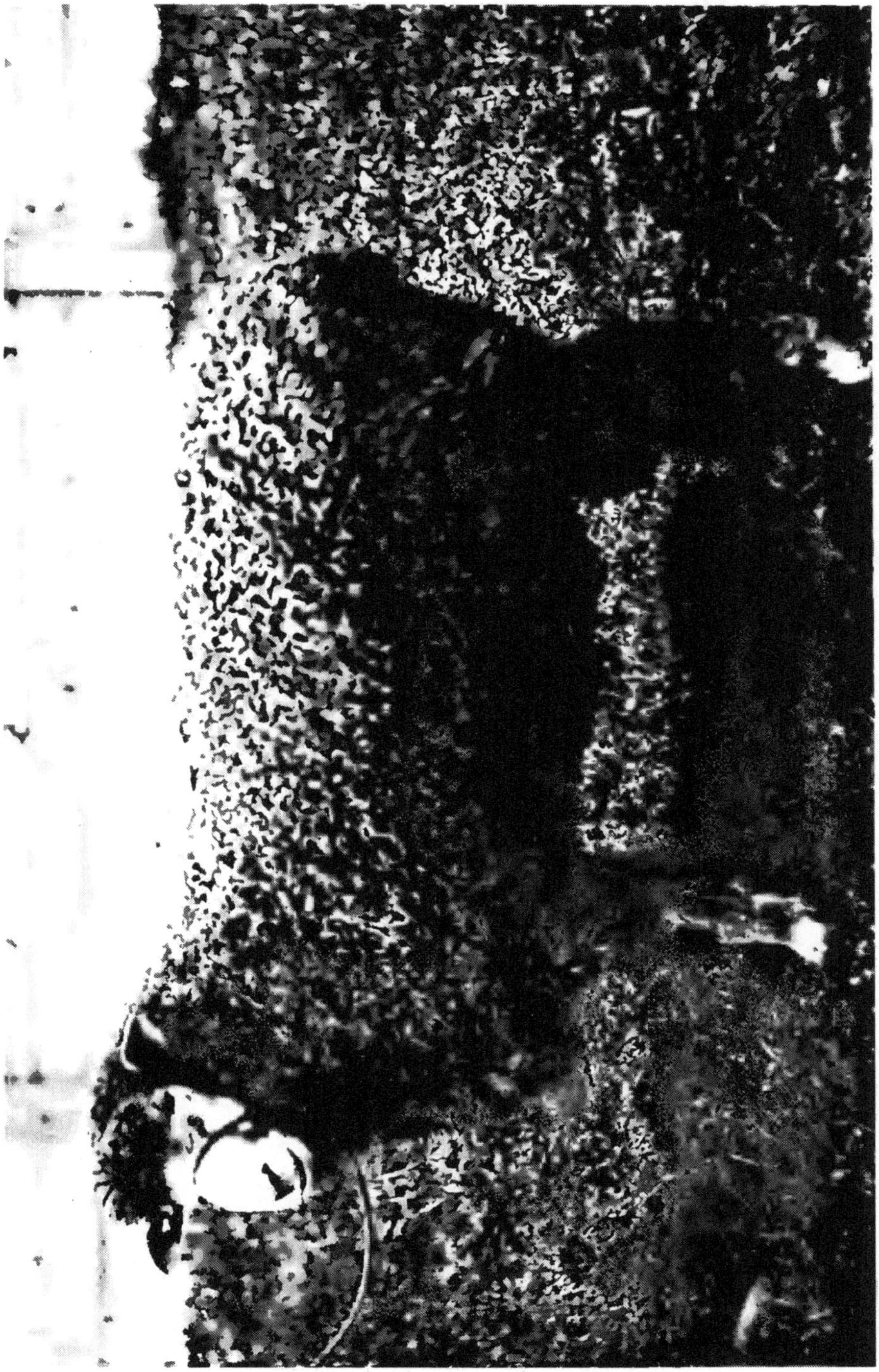

General Management in Disease

part affected, and may attain an enormous weight through tubercular new growth. The tuberculin test is the one usually employed for detecting the disease in cattle and horses.

Cattle may be tubercular, and yet remain in full flesh, but cough and wasting are the general symptoms.

TYMPANITES (*see* Hoven)

U

UDDER, INFLAMMATION OF (GARGET)

This disease affects both cows and ewes, but is commoner in the former. It is also known as Mammitis, and numerous forms of the disease exist, but in a small work of this description these differences are unimportant. Inflammation of the udder may be acute or chronic, curable or incurable. It varies in its course, its causes, and the remedial agents to be employed; therefore it is a difficult task to lay down any particular rules that the amateur can follow. Tuberculosis of the udder is incurable, and is usually denoted by the knotty feeling at the base of the teat.

A frequent cause of garget is exposure of the udder to cold, more especially during calving, there being a physiological congestion at this period which may easily pass into one of disease. It is a painful malady, and often started through imperfect "stripping" during milking. The udder sometimes assumes enormous dimensions, becoming hard, reddened and painful, producing a considerable degree of constitutional disturbance. Treatment should be left to Veterinary Surgeon.

URINE, BLOOD IN (*see* Haematuria)

URTICARIA (OR NETTLE-RASH)

Nettle-rash is a frequent disease in the horse, and may be either acute or chronic. It comes on very suddenly, and sometimes disappears in an equally sudden manner. It is denoted by Pomphi (or Weals), which vary in their size, from a sixpence to a crown, or larger.

Larger weals are formed by confluence, so that large patches of elevated skin occur. The weals may appear on any part of the body. It appears to be due to disturbed digestive functions, and probably impaired nerve force.

Change food: give a dose of purgative medicine, and apply white vinegar and water to the sores.

UTERUS INVERSION OF (*see* Prolapsus Uteri)

V

VERTIGO (GIDDINESS)

This is merely symptomatic of disease. It occurs in sturdy, in louping-ill, and some other diseases.

WILD WHITE CATTLE

General Management in Disease

W

WARTS

These occur in various parts of the body, and are common to most animals. On the tongue, cheeks and mouth; also within the ear and upon the generative organ of the dog; whilst in the horse they are commonest upon the belly and sheath. In cattle, the belly is sometimes literally covered with warts.

To remove them in the dog, dress with Calcined Magnesia or Bismuth. Single warts may be ligatured, but if multiple, they require enucleation.

WIND BROKEN (*see* Broken Wind)

WIND GALLS (*see* Bursal Enlargements)

WEED (LYMPHANGITIS)

Weed, also known as "Shoot of cold," and "Monday morning" disease, is an exceedingly common complaint in the horse.

It comes on suddenly, as a rule, after the animal has stood in the stable for a day or two, following active work; hence the use of the term "Monday morning" disease. It is commonest amongst heavy horses, and one attack predisposes to others. It appears to be a congestion of the lymphatic glands, either under the arm, or of those upon the inner side of the thigh, usually the latter. It is denoted by swelling and tenderness;

the swelling extending from above to below, and the limb may assume enormous dimensions, so that the animal is unable to bend it. Slight fever, and some constitutional disturbance are present as a rule. Treatment: Give exercise; foment the limb with hot water, and consult Veterinary Surgeon.

WORMS

All animals are troubled with intestinal parasites, or worms; and sometimes very severe losses are caused through their presence. Fluke worms, producing liver rot, have already been alluded to (*see* Liver Rot).

Many of these parasites require an intermediate host to complete the cycle of their existence, and the larval form may reside in an animal of a totally different species from that in which the adult parasite resides; thus, for instance, there is a minute worm living in the bowels of the dog, whose larval form takes up its abode in various internal organs in man, horses, cattle and pigs.

Again measles in the pig—which is an affection denoted by minute cysts in the muscles—produces in man a species of tape-worm known as Taenia Solium, whilst beef measles produces another species of tape-worm in the human subject. Sheep suffer from a disease known as vertigo, or sturdy, due to the presence of a bladder-worm locating itself upon the brain, and this is derived

General Management in Disease

from a tape-worm infesting dogs—the ova of which are passed out in the ejecta, and believed to be taken in by sheep during grazing.

Hares and rabbits have also a larval form of tape-worm, and when dogs consume the viscera of these animals, tape-worm may result. All tape-worm are composed of numerous segments, and each segment is endowed with full reproductive powers. These are known as mawworms. Unless the head of the tape-worm is expelled, the animal will still be infested with the parasites. There is a large round worm exceedingly common in the horse, and there may be a gallon of these parasites in the small bowel. It is sometimes nearly 2 feet long, and pointed at each end.

If numerous the worms may block up the canal, and cause death. They are a frequent cause of colic. Numerous species of round worms exist in the horse, and there is one that often produces diarrhoea in colts. This is the four-spined strongyle. In the ox and also in sheep there is a tape-worm known as Taenia expansa, and this occasionally measures 100 feet.

Diarrhoea in sheep, lambs and calves may be caused by worms; so may Bronchitis (*see* Husk, Gapes, etc.).

Several species of tape-worms are common in dogs. There is also a very common round worm known as "Ascaris Marginata," which is a frequent cause of Inflammation of bowels in puppies of only a few days old.

Cats are troubled with corresponding parasites. Birds of all kinds are liable to infestation from worms, both round and flat.

Vermifuges are used for expelling worms, and vermicides for killing them, so that it is better to select a drug having a combined action. Molassine meal is very good for expelling worms in horses and cattle, but there is no worm specific, and this is why a remedy may act in one case but fail in another. Dogs and cats should be kept without food for at least 12 hours before giving worm medicine. In all animals the stomach and bowels should be as empty as possible before the administration of worm medicine. Powdered areca nut is a good remedy for dogs: about a couple of grains for each pound weight of the animal. It should be quite fresh, given in milk, and followed by a purge. Santonin is generally used for round worms, both in horses and dogs. Such drugs as Arsenic, Kamala, Antimony, Aloes, etc., are used as anti-worm remedies, whilst Turpentine and Linseed Oil are frequently given to the horse: a couple of ounces of Turps to $\frac{1}{2}$ pint of Linseed Oil.

Wounds

A wound may be superficial or deep, simple or compound. The situation of the wound and the degree of penetration have an important bearing

General Management in Disease

on the ultimate issue. When the chest, belly, or cranial cavity are opened, the danger is that some important organ may be implicated, and not uncommonly protrude. Pleurisy, Peritonitis, etc., may be induced in this way. Shaft wounds are common in horses, and the severity of such injuries frequently necessitates immediate destruction.

Wounds about the feet of horses are particularly common, whilst broken knee is the commonest accident of all. It varies from the most trifling abrasion down to fracture of the carpal bones. When a wound penetrates into a joint, it gives rise to open-joint and acute inflammation, accompanied by a discharge of joint-oil, which is always a serious condition. Punctured wounds require careful treatment, but it is not always advisable to probe the same, otherwise more damage may be done. The direction of a wound influences its progress; thus, for instance, a wound that passes from below in an upward direction heals quicker than one in the inverse direction, unless artificial drainage be made.

Cattle frequently injure one another with their horns, and lacerations about the female organ are common, and such should be dressed with carbolic glycerine. Infection of a wound commonly occurs at the time of infliction, therefore it is generally advisable to wash it immediately with some antiseptic solution, such as 1 part of Carbolic Acid to 40 parts of water. When a wound is in a state of putrefaction, it ought to be cleansed with a strong solution of Chloride of Zinc—20 grains to every ounce of water. If there is a cavity, rinse it out daily with antiseptic solution.

In every case free drainage is necessary, otherwise the discharge soaks into the muscles, causing softening and destruction of these.

Wounds heal by granulation, and what is termed "proud flesh" merely consists of exuberant granulation, and ought not to be restrained, nor burnt off, unless excessive. Such can be kept back by a pressure bandage.

Some wounds require sewing up, and the materials used for such purposes are, catgut, silk, silver wire, boiled string, etc., whilst blanket pins are frequently used for the same purpose,—the pin being passed through the lip of the wound, and then horse-hair or silk twisted around the ends in figure of 8 fashion.

Deep muscular wounds, in the horse require special forms of suture, but in all external wounds, the sutures are what are termed interrupted, that is, each stitch is taken separately. The stitches must not be adjusted too tightly, otherwise subsequent swelling may tear them out. The margin of the wound should be washed daily, but not the wound itself. In the larger animals the loss of a few quarts of blood is not of much importance, but bleeding can generally be controlled by cold water; by pressure; by tying the bleeding vessels,

General Management in Disease

or by an actual cautery. Wounds about the eyelids and nose require professional skill for their correct adjustment.

During the hot weather, flies trouble a wound, which may become maggoty, and in order to prevent this, smear the wound with an ointment composed of 1 drachm of Oil of Eucalyptus to 2 ounces of Vaseline.

Superficial wounds in the dog may be painted with Friar's Balsam. In conclusion, it must be strongly impressed upon the reader that an apparently trifling wound frequently leads to the most serious consequences, hence the advisability of having recourse to Veterinary skill whenever such is to be had.

YEW-TREE POISONING (*see* Poisoning)

Webster Family Library of Veterinary Medicine
Cummings School of Veterinary Medicine at
Tufts University
200 Westboro Road

CPSIA information can be obtained
at www.ICGtesting.com
Printed in the USA
LVHW060147230320
650872LV00007B/433